LEADING IN A CULTURE OF CHANGE PERSONAL ACTION GUIDE AND WORKBOOK

Leading in a Culture of Change Personal Action Guide and Workbook

Michael Fullan

with Arlette C. Ballew

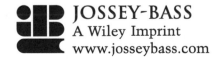

JOSSEY-BASS
A Wiley Imprint
www.josseybass.com

Published by Jossey-Bass
A Wiley Imprint
989 Market Street, San Francisco, CA 94103-1741   www.josseybass.com

Jossey-Bass books and products are available through most bookstores. To contact Jossey-Bass directly call our Customer Care Department within the U.S. at (800) 956-7739, outside the U.S. at (317) 572-3986 or fax (317) 572-4002.

Jossey-Bass also publishes its books in a variety of electronic formats. Some content that appears in print may not be available in electronic books.

ISBN 0-7879-6969-9

Printed in the United States of America
FIRST EDITION
PB Printing   10 9 8 7 6 5 4 3 2 1

CONTENTS

Michael Fullan is a member of the International Centre for Educational Change at the Ontario Institute for Studies in Education at the University of Toronto. He is recognized as an international authority on educational reform. Fullan is engaged in training, consulting, and evaluation of change projects around the world. His ideas for managing change are used in many countries, and his books have been published in many languages. His What's Worth Fighting For trilogy (with Andy Hargreaves), Change Forces trilogy, *The New Meaning of Educational Change,* and *The Moral Imperative of School Leadership* are widely acclaimed.

Arlette C. Ballew is a writer and editor who specializes in experiential learning, training, human resource development, and education. She is coauthor (with Michael Gurian) of *The Boys and Girls Learn Differently Action Guide for Teachers;* coauthor of the seven volumes of Pfeiffer's Training Technologies Series and of *Earthquake Survival: Activities* and *Leader's Guide;* coeditor of the four volumes of *Theories and Models in Applied Behavioral Science;* and developer of many experiential training activities, educational and training packages, leaders' guides, and workbooks. She lives in San Diego, California.

ACKNOWLEDGMENTS

I have benefited enormously from working with colleagues in Toronto and around the world, helping to bring about (and study) large-scale reform. I thank, in particular, Arlette Ballew for her work in using this valuable information and adding to it to create this self-directed workbook.

PREFACE

The more complex society becomes and the more we experience rapid, unpredictable, nonlinear change in our organizations and our world, the more sophisticated leadership must become. Complexity means change, and the pace of change is increasing, as James Gleick, the author who introduced the concept of chaos into popular parlance, points out in *Faster: The Acceleration of Just About Everything* (1999).

Today's leaders face a dilemma: failing to act when the environment is radically changing leads to extinction, yet making quick decisions under conditions of seeming chaos can be equally fatal. Robert Sternberg says: "The essence of intelligence would seem to be in knowing when to think and act quickly, and knowing when to think and act slowly" (cited in Gleick, 1999, p. 114).

If we understand change better, we will be able to influence (but not control) it for the better. This workbook is intended to help leaders and leaders in training to focus on specific, key capabilities that will allow them to lead effectively under conditions of rapid, nonlinear change. It also deals with how to foster leadership in others: to encourage learning, commitment, and responsibility at all levels of the organization—a practice that is needed if our organizations are to survive the challenges of today's complex world.

Knowledge about what creates success under conditions of complexity is getting better. In addition, we have more case examples of large-scale organizational reform and transformation, which yield valuable insights. The information in this workbook draws from experiences in both business and educational organizations. Not surprisingly, there is remarkable convergence in what we are discovering about how to lead in a culture of complex change. No matter what the setting is, leaders and organizations must attend to and develop five core themes, or capabilities, if they are to be successful: moral purpose, understanding change, relationship building, knowledge creation and sharing, and coherence making.

The leadership required in a culture of rapid change is not straightforward. Leaders must be able to operate under complex, uncertain circumstances. Thus, I dedicated *Leading in a Culture of Change* (Fullan, 2001a) to a chaos theory concept: "wildness lies in wait." Bernstein (1996) quotes G. K. Chesterton: "The real trouble with this world of ours is not that it is an unreasonable world, or even that it is a reasonable one. The commonest kind of trouble is that it is nearly reasonable, but not quite. Life is not an illogicality; yet it is a trap for logicians. It looks just a little more mathematical and regular than it is; its exactitude is obvious, but its inexactitude is hidden; its wildness lies in wait" (p. 331).

It's not a bad mantra for leaders in complex times: seek out and honor hidden inexactitudes.

August 2003   Michael Fullan
Toronto, Ontario, Canada

INTRODUCTION

Each chapter of this workbook contains core information from *Leading in a Culture of Change* (Fullan, 2001a), but the content of this workbook is not taken solely from that book. Some materials, particularly those relating exclusively to change in school systems, have been omitted, and new material has been added. In addition, this workbook contains numerous opportunities for reviewing your learning and planning further development. Questions designed to stimulate your application of concepts, techniques, and possibilities to your particular work setting are found throughout the chapters. In each chapter is a variety of lessons to reinforce and allow you to expand your learning, summaries of key points, personal assessment exercises, ideas to discuss with others, and things to try out. The last is particularly important because experimenting and learning in context (that is, in your particular organizational setting) will allow you to become a better leader in that setting. If you work through this book diligently, your new understandings should help in your personal self-development as well as have a beneficial impact on your organizational setting.

Chapter One, "The Five Components of Change Leadership," is an overview of five powerful themes that are deeply compatible and synergistic and are the hallmarks of effective leadership in a time of change: moral purpose, understanding change, building relationships, creating and sharing knowledge, and making coherence.

Chapters Two through Six examine each theme in detail. These five chapters contain a comprehensive theory of leadership. Chapter Seven discusses learning how to become a leader and how systems can foster leadership development. It explains why leadership must be cultivated deliberately over time at all levels of an organization. The appendix contains synopses of points made by leading authors and theorists in a series of books published by Jossey-Bass in 2002. These attest to the validity and usefulness of the concepts and practices presented in this book.

Clearly, a workbook is only as valuable as the effort you put into using it. In attending an experiential learning workshop, you have the opportunity to ask questions, participate in carefully designed learning experiences, learn by interacting with others and trying out new behaviors, observe interactions, and discuss the themes, behaviors, results, and conclusions with those who have gone through a similar experience. Much of this cannot be accomplished in isolation. Therefore, this workbook is designed to encourage you to expand your learning beyond reading and completing the written lessons. In each chapter, you are encouraged to think of ideas and practices to discuss with others and to try out in the real world. Each discussion, each interaction, each behavioral experiment has the potential to serve as the impetus for further learning.

Finally, in the spirit of the values espoused in this workbook, you are encouraged to share your learnings and new skills with others—not by didactic instruction or preaching but by serving as a role model, so that others will be encouraged to ask you questions and seek ways to expand their own leadership capabilities. As Chapter Seven explains, a primary hallmark of effective leaders in a culture of change is the leadership they encourage and develop in others.

LEADING IN A CULTURE OF CHANGE PERSONAL ACTION GUIDE AND WORKBOOK

The Five Components
of Change Leadership

*These days, doing nothing as a leader is a great risk,
so you might as well take the risks worth doing.*

Michael Fullan

Change is a double-edged sword. Its relentless pace is difficult to adjust to, yet when things are unsettled, we can find new ways to move ahead and create breakthroughs that are not possible in stagnant societies. When asked how they feel about change, people often describe anxiety, fear, danger, loss, and panic, as well as excitement, energy, exhilaration, risk taking, and improvement. For better or for worse, change arouses emotions, and when emotions intensify, leadership is key for addressing leadership needs.

LOOKING FOR THE RIGHT KIND OF LEADERSHIP

This book is about leading in a culture of change. It is *not* about being a super-leader. Charismatic leaders inadvertently often do more harm than good because, at best, they provide episodic improvement followed by frustrated or despondent dependence. Superleaders usually are role models who cannot be emulated by most other people, but deep and sustained reform depends on many of us, not just on the extraordinary few.

This book describes key dimensions of leadership that will help any leader, at any level, to guide change better. Every leader can become more effective by focusing on these core aspects of leadership and by developing a new mind-set about a leader's responsibility to himself or herself and to those with whom he or she works.

Leadership and management often overlap, but one difference between them is that leadership is needed for problems that do not have easy answers. The big problems are complex, rife with paradoxes and dilemmas. For these problems, there are no once-and-for-all answers. Yet we expect our leaders to provide solutions. In response, some leaders propose popular, oversimplified solutions. Homer-Dixon (2000) observes that "we demand that [leaders] solve, or at least manage, a multitude of interconnected problems that can develop into crises without warning; we require them to navigate an increasingly turbulent reality that is, in key aspects, literally incomprehensible to the human mind; we buffet them on every side with bolder, more powerful special interests that challenge every innovative policy idea; we submerge them in often unhelpful and distracting information; and we force them to decide and act at an ever faster pace" (p. 15).

---

*Leadership is not mobilizing others to solve problems
we already know how to solve,
but helping them to confront problems
that have not yet been addressed successfully.*

Heifetz (1994) accuses us of looking for the wrong kind of leadership when the going gets tough: "In a crisis . . . we call for someone with answers, decision, strength, and a map of the future, someone who knows where we ought to be going—in short someone who can make hard problems simple. . . . Instead of looking for saviors, we should be calling for leadership that will challenge us to face problems for which there are no simple, painless solutions—problems that require us to learn new ways" (p. 21). Heifetz argues that we should look at the role of the leader as "mobilizing people to tackle tough problems" (p. 15). So leadership is not mobilizing others to solve problems we already know how to solve, but helping them to confront problems that have not yet been addressed successfully.

A FRAMEWORK FOR LEADERSHIP

There is a recent, remarkable convergence of theories, knowledge bases, and strategies that help us to confront complex problems that do not have easy answers. This convergence creates a new mind-set—a framework for thinking about and leading complex change more powerfully than ever before. Figure 1.1 summarizes the framework.

Figure 1.1. A Framework for Leadership

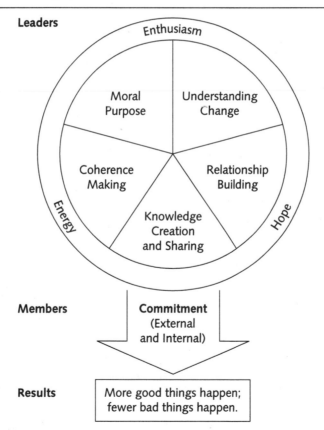

The Five Components of Leadership

There are strong reasons to believe that the five components of leadership presented in *Leading in a Culture of Change* (Fullan, 2001a) and here represent independent but mutually reinforcing forces for positive change:

1. Moral purpose. *Moral purpose* means acting with the intention of making a positive difference in the lives of employees, customers or clients, and society. This is an obvious value with which many of us can identify. Chapter Two explains why there may be inevitable evolutionary reasons that moral purpose will become more prominent and that leaders must be guided by moral purpose to be effective in complex times. Examples from business and education in Chapter Two show that moral purpose is critical to the long-term success of all organizations.

2. Understanding change. It is essential for leaders to *understand the change process.* Moral purpose without an understanding of change will lead to moral martyrdom. Moreover, leaders who combine a commitment to moral purpose with a healthy respect for the complexities of the change process not only will be more successful but also will unearth deeper moral purpose. Understanding of the change process is elusive. The advice in management books often is contradictory, general, confusing, and nonactionable. Chapter Three offers six guidelines that provide leaders with concrete, novel ways of thinking about the process of change: (1) the goal is not to innovate the most; (2) it is not enough to have the best ideas; (3) appreciate the early difficulties of trying something new (this is referred to as the implementation dip); (4) redefine resistance as a potential positive force; (5) reculturing is the name of the game; and (6) never a checklist, always complexity.

3. Building relationships. The one factor common to every successful change initiative is that *relationships* improve. If relationships improve, things get better. If they remain the same or get worse, ground is lost. Therefore, leaders must be consummate relationship builders with diverse people and groups, especially with people different from themselves. Chapter Four tells how effective leaders foster purposeful interaction and problem solving and are wary of easy consensus.

4. Creating and sharing knowledge. The work on *knowledge creation and sharing* reflects an amazing congruence with the previous three themes. We live in the knowledge society, but that term is a cliché. New theoretical and empirical studies of successful organizations examine the operational meaning of the term *knowledge organization.* True leaders commit themselves to continually generating and

increasing knowledge inside and outside the organization. What is astonishing (because it comes from an independent theoretical tradition) is how intimately knowledge relates to the previous three themes. First, people will not voluntarily share knowledge unless they feel some moral commitment to do so; second, people will not share unless the dynamics of change favor exchange; and third, data without relationships merely cause more information glut. Put another way, turning information into knowledge is a social process; for that, you need good relationships. Chapter Five focuses on knowledge building, but we need moral purpose, an understanding of the change process, and good relationships if we are to create and share knowledge.

5. Making coherence. All of this complexity keeps people at the edge of chaos. It is important to be at that edge because that is where creativity resides, but anarchy lurks there too. Therefore, effective leaders tolerate enough ambiguity to keep the creative juices flowing, but along the way (once they and the group know enough), they seek coherence. *Making coherence,* described in Chapter Six, is a perennial pursuit. Leadership is difficult in a culture of change because disequilibrium is common (and valuable, provided that patterns of coherence can be fostered).

Chapters Two through Six present the powerful knowledge base represented by these five components of effective leadership.

In summary, moral purpose is concerned with direction and results; understanding change, building relationships, and knowledge building honor the complexity and discovery of the journey; and coherence making extracts valuable patterns worth retaining. Alas, none of this is quite so linear and fixed as the descriptions of the components.

Energy, Enthusiasm, and Hope

Figure 1.1 shows another set of more personal characteristics that all effective leaders possess: the *energy-enthusiasm-hope* constellation. Energetic, enthusiastic, and hopeful leaders "cause" greater moral purpose in themselves, bury themselves in change, naturally build relationships and knowledge, and seek coherence to consolidate moral purpose. Looking at the dynamic from the other side, we can see that leaders immersed in the five aspects of leadership cannot help feeling and acting more energetic, enthusiastic, and hopeful. Effective leaders make people feel that even the most difficult problems can be tackled productively. They are always hopeful, conveying a sense of optimism and an attitude of never giving up in the pursuit of highly valued goals. Their enthusiasm and confidence (not certainty) are infectious, and the leaders are infectiously effective, provided that they incorporate all five leadership capacities in their day-to-day behavior.

Effective leaders make people feel
that even the most difficult problems
can be tackled productively.

The five capacities operate together in a checks-and-balances fashion. Leaders with deep moral purpose provide guidance, but they also can have blinders if their ideas are not challenged through the dynamics of change, the give-and-take of relationships, and the ideas generated by new knowledge. Similarly, coherence is seen as part of complexity and never can be completely achieved. Leaders in a culture of change value and almost enjoy the tensions inherent in addressing hard-to-solve problems, because that is where the greatest accomplishments lie.

Member Commitment

Figure 1.1 shows how leaders who are steeped in the five core capacities generate long-term commitment in those with whom they work. Effective leaders, because they live and breathe the five aspects of leadership, find themselves committed to staying the course (often they are also inspired by others in the organization as they interact around moral purposes, new knowledge, and the achievement of periodic coherence), and they mobilize more people to be willing to tackle tough problems. By *commitment* we do not mean blind commitment or groupthink, in which a group goes along uncritically with the leader or members adopt the ideas of others in the group. Leaders can be powerful, and so can groups, which means they can be powerfully wrong. This is why the five components of leadership must work in concert: they provide a check against uninformed commitment.

Even when commitment is evidently generated, there are qualifiers. Argyris (2000) helps us make the distinction between external and internal commitment: "These differ in how they are activated and in the source of energy they utilize. External commitment is triggered by management policies and practices that enable employees to accomplish their tasks. Internal commitment derives from energies internal to human beings that are activated because getting a job done is intrinsically rewarding" (p. 40). Argyris notes that "when someone else defines objectives, goals, and the steps to be taken to reach them, whatever commitment exists will be external" (p. 41).

Moral purpose usually is accompanied by a sense of urgency. If a leader is in too much of a hurry, he or she will fail; no one can bulldoze change. More sophisticated leaders may set up systems of pressure and support that will obtain noticeable desired results in the short run, but these will be derived primarily from external commitment. External commitment is still commitment; it is the motivation to put one's effort into the task of change and can be valuable. It can include excitement and the satisfaction of accomplishment and can generate impressive short-term results. But developing internal commitment on a large scale is an extremely difficult proposition.

No one can bulldoze change.

The litmus test of all leadership is whether it mobilizes people's commitment to putting their energy into actions designed to achieve improvements. Individual commitment leads, above all, to collective mobilization. The subsequent chapters show that collective action by itself can be short-lived if it is not based on or does not lead to a deep sense of internal purpose among organizational members. Generating internal over external commitment and external over blind commitment is the sign of effective leadership.

Results

The outcome of effective leadership and commitment is that "more good things happen" and "fewer bad things happen." In business, good things are economic viability, customer or client satisfaction, employee pride, and a sense of being valuable to society. In schools, good things are enhanced student performance, increased capacity of teachers, greater involvement of parents and community members, engagement of students, satisfaction and enthusiasm about going further, and greater pride for all in the system. In both venues, the reduction of bad things means fewer aborted change efforts; less demoralization of employees; fewer examples of piecemeal, uncoordinated reform; and a lot less wasted effort and resources.

DEVELOPING LEADERSHIP

This workbook explores the components of leadership presented in Figure 1.1. It provides insights, strategies, and better theories, knowledge, and action suited to leadership in complex times. In Chapter Seven, it examines how new leaders can be developed. How to foster large numbers of effective leaders in all areas of society is a question that is more pertinent today than ever before. If leadership does not become more attractive, doable, and exciting, public and private institutions will deteriorate. If the experience of rank-and-file members of the organization does not improve, there will not be a pool of potential leaders to cultivate. Good leaders foster good leadership at other levels. Leadership at other levels produces a steady stream of future leaders for the whole system.

Good leaders foster good leadership at other levels.

The conclusion is that leaders will increase their effectiveness if they continually work on the five components of leadership with energy, enthusiasm, and hope: if they pursue moral purpose, understand the change process, develop relationships, foster knowledge building and sharing, and strive for coherence. The rewards and benefits are enormous. It is an exciting proposition. The culture of change beckons.

Key Points

The components of effective leadership are:

- Moral purpose (making a positive difference)
- Understanding change (innovation is not change; there will be an implementation dip; resistance is a potential positive force; reculturing is required; change is complex)

- Relationship building (among diverse people)
- Knowledge creating and sharing (information becomes knowledge through a social process)
- Coherence making (integrating, focusing amid complexity)
- Energy, enthusiasm, hope

These lead to:

- Member commitment (internal and external)
- Results (more good things happen; fewer bad things happen)

Note your reactions to this chapter and any questions it may have generated.

1. In this introductory chapter, what resonated for you or interested you the most?

2. What do you particularly want or need to learn more about?

3. Other comments:

Moral Purpose

*Whatever the enterprise, having moral purpose
makes excellent business sense in the long run.*

Michael Fullan

Some people are deeply passionate about improving life. Others take a more cognitive approach, displaying less emotion but still being intensely committed to betterment. Whatever one's style, every leader, to be effective, must have (and work on improving) moral purpose.

LEADERSHIP AND MORAL PURPOSE

Moral purpose relates to both ends and means. An important end is to make a difference in the lives of customers or clients (internal and external). But the means of getting to that end are also crucial. A leaders who doesn't treat others well and fairly will be a leader without followers. Of course, leading with integrity is not just instrumental. To strive to improve the quality of how we live together is a moral purpose of the highest order.

11

List three people you know, either personally or from history, whom you consider to be authentic leaders—that is, leaders who mobilize others toward high performance with respect to moral purpose. Write several words or phrases that describe each of these people.

Note the commonalities among your descriptions.

In describing this exercise, Sergiovanni (1999) explains what he calls the life-world of leadership:

> Chances are your respondents will mention integrity, reliability, moral excellence, a sense of purpose, firmness of conviction, steadiness, and unique qualities of style and substance that differentiate the leaders they choose from others. Key in this list of characteristics is the importance of substance, distinctive qualities, and moral underpinnings. Authentic leaders anchor their practice in ideas, values, and commitments, exhibit distinctive qualities of style and substance, and can be trusted to be morally diligent in advancing the enterprises they lead. Authentic leaders, in other words, display character, and character is the defining characteristic of authentic leadership [p. 17].

Moral purpose is about how humans evolve over time and especially how they relate to one another. Ridley (1996) and Sober and Wilson (1998) trace the evolution of self-centered and cooperative behavior in animals, insects, and humans. What makes humans different, says Ridley, is culture. Ideas, knowledge, practices, beliefs, and the like enter consciousness and can be passed on "by direct infection from one person to another" (p. 179). Ridley raises the interesting hypothesis that "cooperative groups thrive and selfish ones do not, so cooperative societies have survived at the expense of others" (p. 175). Leaders in all organizations, whether they know it or not, contribute—for better or for worse—to moral purpose in their organizations and in the larger society.

Sober and Wilson (1998) maintain that effective people are driven by self-centered as well as unselfish motives—what they call "motivational pluralism," "both egoistic and altruistic ultimate desires" (p. 308). Most of us have mixed motives, and that is okay. The problem is when, in John Kenneth Galbraith's (2002) words, those in power are engaged in "the search for a superior moral justification for selfishness" (p. 38).

A leader cannot be effective in any setting without behaving in a morally purposeful way. But moral purpose doesn't stand alone. Leaders who work on all five qualities described in this book will find themselves steeped in moral purpose. It will come naturally because it is built into the five components of leadership as they are carried out in practice.

Moral purpose doesn't stand alone.

CASE EXAMPLES

The complexity of pursuing moral purpose in a culture of change can be best illustrated through case examples.

National Literacy and Numeracy Strategy

This example involves twenty thousand schools in England, containing 7 million students up to age eleven. In 1997, the prime minister declared that his three priorities were "education, education, education." The government's goal is to raise the literacy and numeracy (mathematical) achievement of children up to age eleven. It sets specific targets. The percentage of eleven-year-olds scoring 4 or 5 on the test of literacy was 57 percent in 1996 (level 4 being the level at which proficiency standards are met); for numeracy, the baseline was 54 percent. The targets for 2002 were 80 percent for literacy and 75 percent for numeracy. The leaders of the initiative in the Department for Education and Employment set out to "use the change knowledge base" to design a set of pressure-and-support strategies to accomplish this end. They knew they were going to be watched carefully as this highly political and highly explicit initiative unfolded. A team of us at the University of Toronto monitored and assessed the National Literacy and Numeracy Strategy (NLNS).

The main elements of the implementation strategy are summarized by Michael Barber (2000, pp. 8–9), head of the government initiative:

- A nationally prepared project plan for both literacy and numeracy, setting out actions, responsibilities, and deadlines through 2002

- A substantial investment sustained over at least six years and skewed toward those schools that need help most

- A project infrastructure involving national direction from the Standards and Effectiveness Unit, 15 regional directors, and over 300 expert consultants at the local level for each of the two strategies

- An expectation that every class will have a daily math lesson and a daily literacy hour

- A detailed teaching program covering every school year for children from ages 5 to 11

- An emphasis on early intervention and catch up for pupils who fall behind

- A professional-development program designed to enable every primary school teacher to learn to understand and use proven best practices in both curriculum areas

- The appointment of over 2,000 leading math teachers and hundreds of expert literacy teachers who have the time and skill to model best practices for their peers

- The provision of intensive support to half of all schools where the most progress is required

- A major investment in books for schools (over 23 million new books)

- The removal of barriers to implementation (especially a huge reduction in curriculum content outside the core subjects)

- Regular monitoring and extensive evaluation by a national inspection agency

- A national curriculum for initial teacher training that prepares new primary school teachers to teach the daily math lesson and the literacy hour

- A problem-solving philosophy involving early identification of difficulties as they emerge and the provision of rapid solutions or intervention where necessary

- The provision of extra after-school, weekend, and holiday booster classes for those who need extra help to reach the standard

England moved from 57 percent proficient achievement in literacy in 1996 to 75 percent in 2000 and from 54 percent in numeracy in 1996 to 72 percent in 2000. Nevertheless, a preoccupation with achievement scores can have negative side effects, such as narrowing the overall curriculum and burning people out as they relentlessly chase targets.

What are some generic strategies used in the National Literacy and Numeracy Initiative that can be used in other change applications? List them below. (You can find some possible answers at the end of this chapter, but you will learn the most if you do this exercise on your own first.)

This example illustrates the value and dilemmas of moral purpose. Most people see public education as having obvious moral purpose. It improves individual quality of life, fosters social cohesion in a diverse society, and enhances society as a whole. Helping thousands of students to be literate and numerate who otherwise would not be so is not a bad goal. This is bound to make a difference in many lives.

But moral purpose cannot just be stated; it must be accompanied by strategies for realizing it, and those strategies are the leadership actions that energize people to pursue a desired goal. In an interview, Sir Michael Bichard, the permanent secretary at the Department for Education and Employment, said, "For me leadership is about creating a sense of purpose and direction. It's about getting alignment and it's about inspiring people to achieve. . . . [There is a] need to enthuse staff and encourage a belief in the difference their organization is making—whether it is a school or a government department. We can do a lot by making heroes of the people who deliver. It's important to make people feel part of a success story. That's what they want to be" ("Charisma and Loud Shouting," 2000, p. 28).

Of course, pluralistic motives abound. The government wants to be reelected, leaders may get a lot of personal gratification if the strategy is successful, their careers may be enhanced, and there is an explicit measurable purpose.

But is there collateral damage: Do other subjects, such as the arts, suffer? Are educators becoming preoccupied by the test results? Are teachers suffering burnout? Will short-term success be followed by deeper failure? Is the strategy really inspiring principals and teachers to do better? How deep is their commitment?

There are numerous questions about the NLNS. Our conclusion at this stage is that the strategy caught the interest and energy of the majority of principals and teachers and that they were getting a sense of pride and accomplishment from the results so far (Earl and others, 2000). Nevertheless, to use Argyris's terms, the leadership strategy has generated only external commitment on the part of school educators—albeit real commitment that got real results. In order to go deeper, to get at the creative ideas and energies of teachers, additional leadership strategies will be needed to foster internal commitment (commitment activated by intrinsically rewarding accomplishments).

With these possibilities in mind, think about an example from your own knowledge of organizations in which organizational motivation to effect a specific change was primarily external. How might the mobilization of a deeper sense of moral purpose have affected the short-term and long-term outcomes?

In summary, to be effective, leadership has to:

• Have an explicit "making-a-difference" sense of purpose

• Use strategies that mobilize many people to tackle tough problems

• Be held accountable by measured and debatable indicators of success

• Be ultimately assessed by the extent to which it awakens people's intrinsic commitment—the mobilizing of everyone's sense of moral purpose

Finding and communicating the moral imperative of a business may be more difficult. Even when it seems evident to those closest to it, there may be problems, as we shall see.

Monsanto

Pascale, Millemann, and Gioja (2000) report on the case of Monsanto, a life science company that underwent a remarkable transformation between 1993 and 1999 under the direction of a new CEO, Robert Shapiro. Shapiro used a series of "town hall meetings" to introduce a new direction and to begin a dialogue. Pascale, Millemann, and Gioja quote at length from one of Shapiro's presentations in 1995, attended by three hundred of the company's informal leaders:

> Here's what bothers me. There are almost six billion people in the world but the global economy works for only one billion of them. Even for the favored group (and the two billion that are about to join it), there are rising expectations as to the amounts, choice, quality, and health of food. At the other end of the continuum, at least one and a half billion of the world's population are in real trouble. Eight hundred million of these are so malnourished that they cannot participate in work or family life and are on the edge of starvation. Finally, over the next thirty years, most of the additional people joining the planet will be born in poorer places.
>
> The system we have is unsustainable. We burn a lot of hydrocarbons and waste a lot of stuff. There is not enough acreage on earth to provide for humanity's food needs using traditional technology. In developed countries there is the interesting challenge of aging. The elderly consume a lot of health care as technology offers more costly interventions. Fewer people in the workforce end up supporting the higher bill for those who are old. This, too, is politically unsustainable.
>
> Food is shifting from an issue of fuel and calories to an issue of choice. With growing nutritional and environmental consciousness, food must inevitably command a larger share of mind.
>
> These problems for humanity can also be seen as a trillion-dollar opportunity. These are all unresolved problems. It isn't just a question of modular extensions of what we have (via technology and innovations in distribution). We need to reinvent our approach fundamentally. Biotechnology is a profoundly different avenue for agriculture and human health. And information technology provides enough of a difference in degree that it represents a nanotechnology.

Biotechnology is really a subset of information technology. It does not deal with the information that's encoded electronically in silicon but with the information that is encoded chemically in cells, not used for E-mail or spreadsheets but information that tells what proteins to make, when to make them, and how to make them. The rate of increase of knowledge in this field puts Moore's Law to shame, doubling every twelve to eighteen months. We will map the entire human genome by 2005, and will understand most of the functionality of the genome in this same period.

I believe our agriculture and health care systems will be revolutionized by the intersection of biotechnology and information technology. There is something of great consequence in the convergence of these technologies with our market knowledge, and I want you to help me discover what it is [pp. 80–81].

Pascale, Millemann, and Gioja portray the interplay between Shapiro as leader and the employees in this way: "Shapiro points to pieces in the puzzle (life sciences breakthroughs, agriculture, information technology, market knowledge); listeners relate his words to their own experience and fill in the blanks with their detailed knowledge of the business; Shapiro focuses on the unsustainable problems facing humanity—immense challenges that cry out for nontraditional solutions" (p. 81). The authors observe, "Many in the room are moved at the prospect of contributing to the elimination of world hunger and chronic suffering" (p. 83). All this sounds like moral purpose. Ideas, energy, and action involve some ten thousand of Monsanto's thirty thousand employees. Through leadership that mobilized the energies and ideas of employees, Monsanto made a rapid impact in the market. The consulting firm McKinsey called it one of the most thoroughgoing transformations in business history (cited in Pascale, Millemann, and Gioja (2000, p. 86).

Pascale, Millemann, and Gioja note, "Within three years following Monsanto's introduction of genetically modified seeds, farms had shifted 50 percent of all cotton and 40 percent of all soybeans grown in the United States to disease- and herbicide-resistant crops. American cotton growers alone reduced herbicide consumption by $1 billion" (p. 6). Monsanto's share price, they report, "rocketed from $16 to $63" (p. 86).

It would be too simple to conclude that Monsanto was successful. There was growing objection on environmental grounds to genetically modified seeds; Monsanto initially regarded this objection as political backlash and as a public relations problem.

Shapiro and his colleagues still felt that they were making a valuable contribution to the world, but by 1999, Shapiro finally acknowledged (Pascale, Millemann, and Gioja, 2000), "Our confidence in this technology and our enthusiasm for it has, I think, widely been seen, and understandably so, as condescension or indeed arrogance. Because we thought it was our job to persuade, too often we forget to listen" (p. 87).

Today, Monsanto has merged with Upjohn to form Pharmacia, with Shapiro as nonexecutive chairman. It is too early to tell how well Pharmacia will pursue the moral issues embedded in its biotechnology goals. It remains a strong financial competitor.

What are the lessons here? First, a sense of moral purpose on the part of employees is important and can make a huge difference in the performance of the organization. Second, and of growing significance in the global economy, moral purpose applies outside as well as inside the company. Pascale, Millemann, and Gioja (2000) put it this way:

> How a system connects with its external world is also a key source of that system's health. Connectivity is not just about good relations with those outside the company. It impacts the quality of strategy and design and has direct bearing on a company's success.
>
> Biotechnology presents just one example of issues that are too complex to address without a design for broadening the participation of people with diverse concerns and stakes in the questions. Seeking out the views of scientists and government regulators, people affected in different ways by the product, helps everyone imagine and design for unintended consequences. To talk only to oneself as a company will lead to strategic vulnerability [p. 91].

Commitment to the environment and to the broader global community as part of the long-term success of the organization is moral purpose writ large. But in forging ahead with the "why," we cannot afford to forget the "how to" and the "to whom." (Of course, in focusing on the "how to" and the "to whom," we also need to remember the "why.") Pascale, Millemann, and Gioja (2000) conclude, "We can no longer afford to look at our business as atomistic agents alone in a world to which we connect only through competition" (p. 92). Of course, pluralistic motives can coexist: do good, worry about the environment, and derive a profit. But be aware of the interplay of these three forces.

Can you think of another example of an organization that assumed a moral purpose for a change (for example, a policy, procedure, statute, product, or service) that backfired because the organization did not communicate its vision to, and listen to the response of, its clients or customers or others who would be affected? Make some notes here.

Acting with moral purpose in a complex world is, as we have just seen, highly problematic. First, there are many competing priorities (products, services, and outcomes) that cannot all be pursued. Moral purpose means acting with the intention of making a positive difference in the lives of individuals, such as employees and customers or clients, and society. But to achieve the intent of that moral purpose is to forge interaction—and even mutual purpose—across groups, including individuals, organizations, the community, the larger society, and the global society.

*Moral purpose means acting with the intention
of making a positive difference in the lives
of individuals, such as employees and customers
or clients, and society.*

This is why coherence is such an important quality for effective leadership (it is discussed in detail in Chapter Six). Creating coherence, which involves prioritizing and focusing, is greatly facilitated when guided by moral purpose.

Second, and fundamentally, moral purpose is problematic because it must contend with reconciling the diverse interests and goals of different groups: different races, different interest groups (including those who may have a vested interest in the status quo as long as it works in their favor), different power bases, and people from different lots in life.

Key Points About Leadership and Moral Purpose

1. Every leader, to be effective, must have moral purpose.

2. Moral purpose relates to both ends and means. The means are also crucial.

3. Authentic leaders have distinctive style and substance and moral underpinnings (ideas, values, and commitments). They are morally diligent in advancing the enterprises they lead. They display character—the defining characteristic of authentic leadership.

4. Cooperative groups thrive, and selfish ones do not.

5. Most people have "both egoistic and altruistic ultimate desires," and that's okay.

6. To be effective, leadership has to

   • Have an explicit "making-a-difference" sense of purpose

   • Use strategies that mobilize many people to tackle tough problems

   • Be held accountable by measured and debatable indicators of success

   • Be ultimately assessed by the extent to which it awakens people's intrinsic commitment—the mobilizing of everyone's sense of moral purpose

7. Moral purpose cannot just be stated. It must be accompanied by strategies for realizing it, and those strategies are the leadership actions that energize people to pursue a desired goal.

8. Change mandated from the top down (external commitment) can result in burnout.

9. It is important to help the people who carry out the strategies to feel part of a success story.

ORGANIZATIONS AND MORAL PURPOSE

Profit-minded organizations do better when they pay attention to moral purpose. De Gues worked for Royal Dutch/Shell for almost forty years and studied "long-living companies." He found that in many countries, 40 percent of newly created companies last less than ten years and that even "the big solid companies" do not hold out for more than an average of forty years (p. 2). By contrast, long-lived companies (those lasting more than fifty years) have a strong sense of purpose and are adaptive to their environments without compromising core ideals.

De Gues talks about both the negative and the positive case: "Companies die because their managers focus on the economic activity of producing goods and services, and they forget their organizations' true nature is that of a community of humans" (p. 3). In contrast are healthy living companies, which

> will have members, both humans and other institutions, who subscribe to a set of common values and who believe that the goals of the company allow them and help them to achieve their own individual goals. Both the company and its constituent members have basic driving forces; they want to survive, and once the conditions for survival exist, they want to reach and expand their potential. The underlying contract between the company and its members (both individuals and other institutions) is that the members will be helped to reach their potential. It is understood that this, at the same time, is in the company's self-interest. The self-interest of the company stems from its understanding that the members' potential helps create the corporate potential [p. 200].

Whatever the enterprise, having moral purpose—in terms of both contribution to society and development of commitment in employees—makes excellent business sense in the middle to long run. Organizations without such purpose die sooner rather than later. At best, they win the occasional early battle and steadily lose the war.

The message of this chapter is that moral purpose is worthwhile on just about every meaningful criterion; it may not become activated on its own accord, but it is there in nascent form to be cultivated and activated. Moral purpose has a tendency to surface and become stronger as humankind evolves (Fullan, 1999). Effective leaders exploit this tendency and make moral purpose a natural ally. Although moral purpose is natural, it will flourish only if leaders cultivate it.

Although moral purpose is natural,
it will flourish only if leaders cultivate it.

There are signs that moral purpose is on the ascendance in schools and businesses. In *The Courage to Teach* (1998), Palmer tells how the best teachers integrate the intellectual, emotional, and spiritual aspects of teaching to create powerful learning communities. Similarly, Garten (2001) interviewed forty prominent men and women around the world who held CEO, president, or chairperson positions in major companies. He describes how some executives have made the direct link between social responsibility and the morale, productivity, and loyalty of employees. He quotes Jarma Ollila, chairman and CEO of Nokia Corporation:

> People want their company to be a good citizen. They want it to show true concern for the world, for the environment. They want it to have a social conscience. There is now a very clear expectation which is coming from political life as well as our employees, that companies will have to have a soul, a state of mind which represents a social conscience. That's very different from the early 1990s when we were applauded just for employing more people. There is a very high expectation, something I did not see when I started as CEO in 1992 [p. 184].

Similarly, Bolman and Deal (2000) predict that "culture and core values will be increasingly recognized as the vital social glue that infuses an organization with passion and purpose. Workers will increasingly demand more than a paycheck. They'll want to know the higher calling or enabling purpose of their work" (p. 185).

However, Garten (2001) adds that most leaders fail "to see the gap between society's expectations of what they should do and what they seem prepared to do" (p. 192).

Key Points About Organizations and Moral Purpose

1. Moral purpose is a key element in the sustainability of organizations. Long-lived companies have a strong sense of purpose and are adaptive to their environments without compromising core ideals.

2. Healthy organizations help their members to expand their potential and achieve their individual goals. This is in the organization's self-interest and helps to create the organization's potential.

3. Increasingly, moral purpose is what infuses an organization with passion and purpose. Workers want to know the enabling purpose of their work.

The most fundamental conclusion of this chapter is that moral purpose and sustained performance of organizations are mutually dependent. Pascale, Millemann, and Gioja (2000) found elements of this kind of leadership in the seven companies they studied and call "sustainability" the challenge of the century: "The theory of sustainability is that it is constituted by a trinity of environmental soundness, social justice, and economic viability. If any of these three are weak or missing, the theory of sustainability says that that practice [what the organization is doing] will not prove sustainable over time" (p. 92).

In a culture of change, it is easy to lose one's way, even if one is motivated by moral purpose. Moral purpose without an understanding of change will lead to moral martyrdom. Leaders who combine a commitment to moral purpose with a healthy respect for the complexities of the change process will be more successful and will unearth deeper moral purpose. The next chapter tells why understanding the change process is necessary for all leaders.

In this chapter, what resonated for you? Note your reactions to this chapter, any insights or questions it may have generated, or any specific things you might want to refer to later.

Lessons from the Monsanto Case Example

Write your answers to the questions that follow.

1. What were the key points (lessons) from the example of Monsanto? Make some notes below.

2. Did you think of examples of other organizations that produced policies, procedures, statutes, products, services, or other changes that had "moral purpose" but created backlash in the marketplace? (Here are a few examples to stimulate your thinking: the electric car, the "morning-after" pill, specific laws or regulations.) If you made notes previously, refer to them now. If you didn't, make some notes here.

3. What do the examples tell you about the need to identify and communicate with a variety of stakeholders and groups outside the organization?

Key Points from the Monsanto Case Example

1. How a system connects with its external world is a key indicator of that system's health.

2. Before planning change, it is important to identify and engage the participation of people and groups who may be concerned with or affected by the change. To achieve moral purpose is to forge interaction across these groups.

3. It is important to use the input of these individuals and groups in order to help everyone imagine and design for unintended consequences. To talk only inside the organization will lead to strategic vulnerability.

4. Nearsighted moral purpose may be seen as arrogance or worse.

Your Personal Assessment

Write your answers to the questions that follow.

1. What is your own moral purpose in your work?

2. How would you explain this to your friends, customers or clients, and community?

3. How do you think others perceive you in terms of moral purpose? Does this differ in your private life and your work life? If so, how?

4. How well do you think you measure up as a leader in terms of moral purpose?

5. What do you need to work on in terms of your own capacities as a leader in regard to moral purpose?

6. Does your organization have a stated moral purpose (for example, in its mission statement or vision statement)? If so, what is it? If not, what do you think is the moral purpose of your organization, if any? What does your organization (or division) stand for? What does it contribute to the community or to society? How does it make a difference? What will its legacy be?

7. How would you explain your organization's moral purpose, meaning, contribution or difference to your friends, customers and clients, and members of your community?

8. Whether stated or not, what higher-order purpose actually motivates people in your organization (for example, knowledge or skill development, recycling, preservation of natural resources, coaching and development of others, honesty, being able to give input and make decisions about the work they do)?

9. How can this be tapped or harnessed as a motivator for change?

Things to Discuss with Others

Talking about these issues with others helps you to widen the lens. What have you learned in this chapter that you might discuss with specific others, to your developmental benefit?

 ## Things to Try Out

ANSWERS: Lesson from the Example of the National Literacy and Numeracy Strategy

Here are some strategies that can be translated to other change efforts (you may have worded these differently, and that's fine):

Structure

- A plan that sets out actions, responsibilities, and deadlines
- A substantial investment, skewed toward the sectors that need the most help
- Detailed expectations and programs to achieve them
- Removal of barriers to implementation
- Regular monitoring and extensive evaluation

Development and Support

- A project infrastructure involving overall leadership and expert consultants at local levels
- A professional development program that includes best practices
- Modeling of best practices by high achievers
- Provision of support and needed materials
- Training in the new standards and practices
- A problem-solving philosophy involving early identification of problems and difficulties and the provision of rapid solutions or interventions

Understanding Change

*Although change is unpredictable,
you can set up conditions that help to guide the process.*

Michael Fullan

Change is rapid and nonlinear, which creates messiness. It also offers great potential for creative breakthroughs. The paradox is that transformation would not be possible without the messiness.

Most change in any system occurs as a response to disturbances in the system's external or internal environment. If the response to the disturbance is immediate and reflexive, it often is unmanaged, and other problems often arise as a result. However, problems also arise when one attempts to "manage" change.

SEVERAL VIEWS OF CHANGE

People need pressure or a compelling reason to change. Kurt Lewin (1947) noted that most people are "frozen" in terms of their openness to change. He described the initiation of change as "unfreezing," which is followed by the change, and then by "refreezing," that is, using the changed habits, behaviors, procedures, or materials in place of the old ones. Unfreezing may be a natural response to an immediate need, or it may be a process that those who espouse a particular change attempt to dictate.

According to Havelock (1973), planned, problem-solving change has five steps:

1. Feeling a need and deciding to do something about it

2. Attempting to define the problem

3. Searching for promising solutions

4. Applying one or more promising solutions to the need

5. Determining whether the problem is solved satisfactorily and repeating the problem-solving cycle if it is not

Unfortunately, this pattern often generates problems of its own. First, attempting to define the problem is usually done at the executive level or by outside consultants rather than by the people who live with the problem at work or will have to live with the implied change. Second, few organizations today have the luxury of applying a "promising" solution, determining whether it solved the problem (as defined), and repeating the cycle if it did not (we do not know how many times the cycle is assumed to be repeated until the correct solution is found). Imagine the disruption to the organizational system during this process. Another problem is the tacit assumption that change can be directed and orderly. Much of the early literature on organizational change reflected this assumption; individuals and systems that did not change in the prescribed manner were labeled "resistant."

We have been inundated with complex and often unclear or contradictory advice about how to effect organizational change. Would you know what to do if you read Kotter's eight-step process (1996, p. 21) for initiating top-down transformation?

1. Establishing a sense of urgency
2. Creating a guiding coalition
3. Developing a vision and strategy
4. Communicating the change vision
5. Empowering broad-based action
6. Generating short-term wins
7. Consolidating gains and producing more change
8. Anchoring new approaches in the culture

Would you still know what to do if you then turned to Beer, Eisenstat, and Spector's advice (1990) about drawing out bottom-up ideas and energies?

1. Mobilize commitment to change through joint diagnosis [with people in the organization] of business problems.
2. Develop a shared vision of how to organize and manage for competitiveness.
3. Foster concerns for the new vision, competence to enact it, and cohesion to move it along.
4. Spread revitalization to all departments without pushing it from the top.
5. Institutionalize revitalization through formal policies, systems, and structure.
6. Monitor and adjust strategies in response to problems in the revitalization process.

Or what about Hamel's advice (2000) to "lead the revolution" by being your own seer?

Step 1: Build a point of view.
Step 2: Write a manifesto.
Step 3: Create a coalition.
Step 4: Pick your targets and pick your moments.
Step 5: Co-opt and neutralize.
Step 6: Find a translator.
Step 7: Win small, win early, win often.
Step 8: Isolate, infiltrate, integrate.

For example, should you emphasize top-down or bottom-up strategies? Argyris (2000) calls this type of thing "unactionable advice" (p. 15).

Egan (1988a, 1988b) was one of the first to note the "messiness" (arational factors) inherent in organizations. For example, strategy and operations are not always well integrated; individuals within the system have different idiosyncrasies, approaches, and problems; cliques and friendships or animosities affect the functioning of subsystems; and political factors, such as power and authority, protection of turf, and competition for resources, exist. The organizational culture, which affects and is affected by the previously named factors, can greatly enhance or inhibit the system's effectiveness. In Stage I of his change model, Egan calls for vigilance throughout the organization in monitoring emerging problems and opportunities, challenging blind spots, seeking points of leverage, and gathering clear and specific action-oriented data. His Stage II entails defining what the organization needs and wants but not how it is to be achieved. It involves brainstorming possibilities and evaluating them in terms of realism, adequacy, fit with the organizational culture, and consequences. It includes getting commitment from key stakeholders. In Stage III, a wide range of strategies is proposed, and organizational players determine what steps need to be taken and in what order. Note that Egan places the responsibility for change deep within the organization and considers the key stakeholders and the organizational culture to be primary considerations. We expand on this view in later chapters.

As our understanding of organizational change has increased, many of us have concluded that change cannot be "managed." It can be understood, and perhaps led, but it cannot be fully controlled. After taking us through ten management schools of thought, Mintzberg, Ahlstrand, and Lampel (1998) draw the conclusion that "the best way to 'manage' change is to allow for it to happen" (p. 324), "to be pulled by the concerns out there rather than being pushed by the concepts in here" (p. 373). This is perhaps an overstatement, but leadership can make a difference—not just by having good ideas but in particular by understanding the processes of change. Strong change processes help good ideas to become embedded.

---

*Change cannot be "managed." It can be understood,
and perhaps led, but it cannot be fully controlled.*

Our purpose is to understand change in order to lead it better. The list that follows summarizes this chapter's contribution to understanding the change process. As with the five components in Figure 1.1, the goal is to develop a greater sense for leading complex change, to develop a mind-set and action set that are continually cultivated and refined. There are no shortcuts.

Key Points About Change

1. Change is rapid and nonlinear, which creates messiness. It also offers great potential for creative breakthroughs. The paradox is that transformation would not be possible without the messiness.

2. Most change in any system occurs as a response to disturbances in the system's external or internal environment. If the response to the disturbance is immediate and reflexive, it often is unmanaged, and other problems can arise as a result. Problems also arise when one attempts to "manage" change.

3. Arational factors in organizations include strategy and operations that are not well integrated; different individual idiosyncrasies, approaches, and problems; friendships and animosities that affect the functioning of subsystems; and political factors, such as power and authority, protection of turf, and competition for resources.

4. Key stakeholders and the organizational culture are primary considerations in organizational change.

5. Change cannot be "managed" (controlled). It can be understood and perhaps led.

LEADERSHIP STYLE AND CHANGE

Goleman (2000) analyzed a database from a random sample of 3,871 executives from the consulting firm Hay/McBer. He examined the relationships between leadership style, organizational climate, and financial performance. Climate was measured by combining six factors of the working environment: flexibility, responsibility, standards, rewards, clarity, and commitment. Financial results included return on sales, revenue growth, efficiency, and profitability.

Following are the six leadership styles Goleman identified (pp. 82–83):

1. Coercive: the leader demands compliance. ("Do what I tell you.")
2. Authoritative: the leader mobilizes people toward a vision. ("Come with me.")
3. Affiliative: the leader creates harmony and builds emotional bonds. ("People come first.")
4. Democratic: the leader forges consensus through participation. ("What do you think?")

5. Pacesetting: the leader sets high standards for performance. ("Do as I do, now.")
6. Coaching: the leader develops people for the future. ("Try this.")

Two of the six styles negatively affected climate and, in turn, performance: the coercive style (people resent and resist) and the pacesetting style (people get overwhelmed and burn out). All four of the other styles had a significant positive impact on climate and performance.

With an understanding that leadership affects climate and performance, let us now examine some truths about the change process.

UNDERSTANDING THE CHANGE PROCESS

- The goal is not to innovate the most.

- It is not enough to have the best ideas.

- Appreciate the implementation dip.

- Redefine resistance.

- Reculturing is the name of the game.

- Never a checklist, always complexity.

The Goal Is Not to Innovate the Most

The organization or leader who takes on the most innovations is not the winner. In education, such organizations are called "Christmas tree schools" (Bryk and others, 1998): they glitter from a distance, but the superficial decorations lack depth and coherence.

Goleman's (2000) pacesetter leader relentlessly takes on innovation after innovation:

> The leader sets extremely high performance standards and exemplifies them himself. He is obsessive about doing things better and faster, and he asks the same of everyone around him. He quickly pinpoints poor

performers and demands more from them. If they don't rise to the occasion, he replaces them with people who can. You would think such an approach would improve results, but it doesn't. In fact, the pacesetting style destroys climate. Many employees feel overwhelmed by the pacesetter's demands for excellence, and their morale drops—guidelines for working may be clear in the leader's head, but she does not state them clearly; she expects people to know what to do [p. 86].

Can you think of a real-life example of a pacesetter leader? What is (or was) the effect of this leader on organizational performance and morale?

The pacesetter often ends up being a "lone ranger," as Peter Negroni (quoted in Senge and others, 2000) put it in reflecting on his experience (and his eventual change to lead learner). During the first three years in which Negroni was school superintendent in Springfield, Massachusetts, his overall goal was "to change this inbred system": "Intent on the ends, I operated as Lone Ranger. I didn't try to build relationships with the teachers' union or with the board. Instead, I worked around them. Most of the time, I felt that I was way out in front of them. I would change things on my own" (p. 426). For all the changes he pushed through, he says, "these were three brutal years for all of us. . . . I was running so fast and making so many changes that I was getting tired. People around me were even more sick and tired" (pp. 426–427).

The pacesetter often ends up being a "lone ranger."

Eventually, through reflective practice and feedback, Negroni moved to transforming the district into a learning institution. He explains (quoted in Senge and others, 2000):

> Our most critical role at the central office is to support learning about learning, especially among principals—who will then do the same among teachers in their schools. At the beginning of the year, three or four central office administrators and I conducted forty-six school visits in forty-six days, with the principals of each school alongside us. Then the administrators and all forty-six principals met together to summarize what we had seen. This is one of a series of walk-throughs that principals do during the course of a school year—with me, with other central office administrators, and with each other. The sequence includes a monthly "grand round," when every principal in the district goes with me and the eight academic directors to spend the day in one school. We break up into subgroups for hour-and-a-half visits, then come back and (still in subgroups) discuss what we saw. Then a representative from each subgroup makes a presentation to all of the principals [p. 431].

If you are in an organization other than a school, rewrite the process described above to make it a possible process of visitation, observation, learning, and sharing in your organization.

These principals are deeply engaged in innovation, but it is less frenetic and more organically built into the culture. Pacesetters must learn the difference between competing in a change marathon and developing the capacity and commitment to solve complex problems. It is important that a leader not assume that his or her version of what a change should be is one that should or could be implemented. No one can mandate what matters. Leaders can legislate reform but cannot mandate ownership and implementation. Any significant innovation, if it is to result in true change, requires individual implementers to work out their own meaning.

It Is Not Enough to Have the Best Ideas

The leader who has some of the best ideas around but can't get anyone to buy into them may be dead right. She often experiences overwhelming opposition. Goleman (2000) describes a coercive leader who was called in to help a computer company that was in crisis mode: "He set to work chopping jobs, selling off divisions and making the tough decisions that should have been executed years before. The company was saved, at least in the short-term" (p. 82). Before long, however, morale plummeted, and the short-term success was followed by another, less recoverable, downturn.

Even the more sophisticated versions of "having good ideas" are problematic. Pascale, Millemann, and Gioja (2000) call these leaders social engineers:

> Corporations around the world now write checks for more than $50 billion a year in fees for "change consulting." And that tab represents only a third of the overall change cost if severance costs, write-offs, and information technology purchases are included. Yet, consultants, academic surveys, and reports from "changed" companies themselves indicate that a full 70 percent of those efforts fail. The reason? We call it *social engineering,* a contemporary variant of the machine model's cause-and-effect thinking. *Social* is coupled with *engineering* to denote that most managers today, in contrast to their nineteenth-century counterparts, recognize that people need to be brought on board. But they still go about it in a preordained fashion. Trouble arises because the "soft" stuff is really the *hard* stuff, and no one can really "engineer" it [p. 12].

Having good ideas is not a bad thing. It is an element of effective leadership, as in Goleman's authoritative style. Goleman (2000) describes a vice president of marketing at a floundering national restaurant chain that specialized in pizza: "[Tom] made an impassioned plea for his colleagues to think from the customer's perspective. . . . The company was not in the restaurant business, it was in the business of distributing high-quality, convenient-to-get pizza. That notion—and nothing else—should drive what the company did. . . . With his vibrant enthusiasm and clear vision—the hallmarks of the authoritative style—Tom filled a leadership vacuum at the company" (p. 83).

Goleman's data show that the authoritative leader had a positive impact on climate and performance. So do we need a leader with a clear vision who can excite and mobilize people to committing to it, or don't we? The answer is a bit complicated. In some situations, as when there is an urgent problem and people are muddled, visionary leaders can be crucial. It always helps when leaders have good ideas. But it is easy for authoritative leadership to slip into social engineering when the initial excitement cannot be sustained because it cannot be converted to internal commitment.

Authoritative leaders need to recognize the weaknesses as well as the strengths in their approach. They need, as Goleman concludes, to use all four of the successful leadership styles: "Leaders who have mastered four or more—especially the authoritative, democratic, affiliative, and coaching styles—have the best climate and business performance" (p. 87).

Authoritative leaders need to recognize the weaknesses as well as the strengths in their approach.

Appreciate the Implementation Dip

One of our most consistent findings about the change process is that successful organizations experience implementation dips as they move forward (Fullan, 2001b). The implementation dip is a dip in performance and confidence as one engages in an innovation that requires new skills and new understandings. All innovations worth their salt call on people to question and, in some respects, to change their behaviors and their beliefs—even when innovations are pursued voluntarily.

*Successful organizations experience
implementation dips as they move forward.*

How do you feel when you find yourself not being proficient and needing new skills (when you have been used to knowing what you are doing)?

This kind of experience is classic change material. People feel anxious, fearful, confused, overwhelmed, deskilled, cautious, and—if they have moral purpose—deeply disturbed. Because we are talking about a culture of rapid change, there is no shortage of implementation dips—or even chasms. Black and Gregersen (2002) found that some people prefer to do the old "wrong" thing competently rather than the new "right" thing incompetently. This is the implementation dip, and leaders need to help people work through the early anxieties of change:

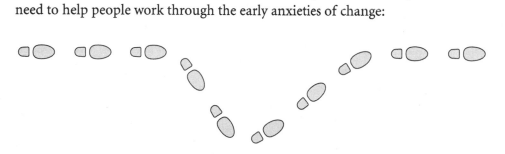

Pacesetters and coercers have no empathy for people who are undergoing implementation dips. Effective leaders have sensitivity to implementation. They know that change is a process, not an event. They don't panic when things don't go smoothly during the first year of a major change or new direction. They are empathic to the lot of people immersed in the anxiety-ridden work of trying to bring about a new order. They are even, as we discuss below, appreciative of resistance.

Leaders who understand the implementation dip know that people are experiencing two kinds of problems when they are in the dip: the social-psychological fear of change and the lack of technical know-how to make the change work. It should be obvious that leaders need affiliative and coaching styles in these situations. The affiliative leader pays attention to people, focuses on building emotional bonds, builds relationships, and heals rifts. The coaching leader helps people to develop and invests in their capacity building (Goleman, 2000).

Some elements of authoritative leadership help. Enthusiasm, self-confidence, optimism, and clarity of vision all can inspire people to keep going. The problems start when a leader is only authoritative or only affiliative or only a coach. Leaders who are sensitive to the implementation dip combine styles: they still have an urgent sense of moral purpose and they still measure success in terms of results, but they do things that are more likely to get the organization going and keep it going.

Redefine Resistance

We are more likely to learn something from people who disagree with us than we are from people who agree. But we tend to hang around with and listen to people who agree with us, and we prefer to avoid and not listen to those who do not. This may be a good strategy for getting through the day, but it is a lousy one for getting through the implementation dip.

We are more likely to learn something from people who disagree with us.

Pacesetters and coercers are terrible listeners, and authoritative leaders are not that good at listening. Affiliative and democratic leaders listen too much. This is why leadership is complicated: it requires combining elements that do not easily go together. Leaders should have good ideas and present them well (the authoritative element) while seeking and listening to doubters (aspects of democratic leadership). They must try to build good relationships (be affiliative) even with those who may not trust them.

The conflict and disagreement that accompany the work of change are inevitable and fundamental to successful change. Chapter Four presents the complexities of resistance and its unappreciated positive side. Suffice it to say here that we need to respect resisters for two reasons. First, they sometimes have ideas that we might have missed, especially in situations of diversity or complexity or in the tackling of problems for which the answer is unknown. Maurer (1996) says, "Often those who resist have something important to tell us. We can be influenced by them. People resist for what they view as good reasons. They may see alternatives we never dreamed of. They may understand problems about the minutiae of implementation that we never see from our lofty perch atop Mount Olympus" (p. 49).

Second, resisters are crucial when it comes to the politics of implementation. In democratic organizations, being alert to differences of opinion is absolutely vital. In all organizations, respecting resistance is essential; if you ignore it, it is only a matter of time before it takes its toll—during implementation, if not earlier. In even the most tightly controlled and authority-bound organization, it is easy to sabotage new directions during implementation. Even when things appear to be working, the apparent success may be a function of merely superficial compliance.

Respecting resistance is essential.

For all these reasons, successful leaders not only encourage like-minded innovators; they deliberately build in differences. They don't mind so much when others—not just themselves—disturb the equilibrium. They also trust the learning process they set up: focusing on moral purpose; attending to the change process; building relationships; creating, sharing, and critically scrutinizing knowledge; and traversing the edge of chaos while seeking coherence. Successful organizations and their leaders know that these dynamics contain just about all the checks and balances needed to deal with those few hard-core resisters who make a career out of being against everything—who act without moral purpose.

Reculturing Is the Name of the Game

Most organizations today have been or will be "reorganized (that is, their structures and organizational charts are changed, but their cultures and actions are not). Almost two thousand years ago, Gaius Petronious said (cited in Gaynor, 1977), "We trained hard . . . but it seemed every time we were beginning to form up into teams we were reorganized. I was to learn later in life that we tend to meet any situation by reorganizing, and what a wonderful method it can be for creating the illusion of progress while producing confusion, inefficiency, and demoralization" (p. 28).

Structure does make a difference, but it is not the main point in achieving success. Transforming the culture—changing the way things are done—is the main point. I call this *reculturing*. Effective leaders know that the hard work of reculturing is the sine qua non of progress. Furthermore, it is a particular kind of reculturing for which we strive: one that activates and deepens moral purpose through collaborative work cultures that respect differences and continually build and test knowledge against measurable results—a culture within which one realizes that sometimes being off balance is a learning moment.

Leading in a culture of change means creating a culture (not just a structure) of change. It does not mean adopting one innovation after another; it means producing the capacity to seek, critically assess, and selectively incorporate new ideas and practices—all the time, and inside the organization as well as outside it.

Reculturing involves hard, labor-intensive work. It takes time and it really never ends. This is why successful leaders need energy, enthusiasm, and hope and why they need moral purpose along with the other four leadership capacities. Later we present case examples of reculturing, because it is part of developing relationships (Chapter Four), creating knowledge (Chapter Five), and striving for coherence in a nonlinear world (Chapter Six).

Reculturing takes time and it really never ends

Never a Checklist, Always Complexity

It is no doubt clear by now that there never can be a recipe for change, that is, a step-by-step process. Even seemingly sophisticated plans like Kotter's (1996) or Hamel's (2000) eight steps are suspect if used as the basis for planning, although they may be useful to stimulate thinking. It is more productive to develop your own mind-set based on the five core components of leadership, because you are more likely to internalize what makes for effective leadership in complex times. This makes it difficult for leaders, because they will be pushed to provide solutions. In times of urgent problems and confusing circumstances, people demand leaders who can show the way. (Just try explaining to your board of directors that you have based your strategic plan on the properties of nonlinear feedback networks and complex adaptive systems.) In other words, leaders and members of the organization, because they live in a culture of frenetic change, are vulnerable to seeking the comforting clarity of off-the-shelf solutions. If one doesn't work, there will be another one next year. As stated in Chapter Two, interaction with and information from the wider environment are critical for success, and no off-the-shelf solution can supply that. The trap is that the more complex and urgent the situation is, the more people look for off-the-shelf solutions.

Effective leaders must cultivate their understanding of and skills in what is known as complexity science. (For the best discussion of this subject, see Pascale, Millemann, and Gioja, 2000; and Stacey, 2000; see also Fullan, 1993, 1999, 2003a). Complexity science is one of those remarkable convergences of independent streams of inquiry referred to in Chapter One. This science, as Pascale, Millemann, and Gioja (2000) claim, grapples with the mysteries of life and living; it is producing exciting new insights into life itself and how we might think about organizations, leadership, and social change. "Living systems [like businesses] cannot be *directed* along a linear path. Unforeseen consequences are inevitable. The challenge is to *disturb* them in a manner that approximates the desired outcomes" (p. 6).

Leaders must resist the temptation to try to control the uncontrollable and use concepts from complexity theory to design and guide learning and change. Although change is unpredictable, you can set up conditions that help to guide the process. In complexity theory, "order emerges naturally because of unpredictable interaction" (Marion, 1999, p. xii). When two or more entities interact, they influence one another. Marion also notes that "chaotic systems flit a bit too readily from novelty to novelty; living systems need to consolidate gains. Predictable, stable systems, by contrast, possess none of the panache needed to create new order or even to respond adaptively to creature environments. Complex systems lie between these poles, at the edge of chaos; and they have both panache and stability sufficient to serve life" (p. xiv).

Leaders must resist the temptation to try to control the uncontrollable.

Core concepts of complexity theory include the following (Fullan, 2003a):

- Equilibrium is a precursor to death. When a living system is in a state of equilibrium, it is not prepared to respond to changes in its environment in ways that will enable it to survive. In the face of threat, it is unprepared.

- A complex adaptive system has high degrees of internal interaction as well as external interaction with other systems in a way that creates continual learning.

- As systems interact, they influence one another, correlate, and move toward new patterns.

- Change is non-linear; reforms do not unfold as intended.

- Change is unpredictable; surprises occur as a result of dynamically complex interactive forces.

Rewrite the five concepts above in your own words. This exercise will help you to remember them.

1.

2.

3.

4.

5.

Key Points About Complexity Science

1. Stagnant systems cannot respond adaptively to their environments. When a living system is in a state of equilibrium, it is not prepared to respond to changes in or threats from its environment in ways that will enable it to survive.

2. Interaction with and information from the environment are critical. A complex adaptive system has high degrees of internal interaction as well as external interaction with other systems in a way that creates continual learning.

3. Complex systems have both the ability to respond adaptively and the stability needed to enable them to survive.

4. As systems interact, they influence one another, correlate, and move toward new patterns.

5. Change is unpredictable. Living systems cannot be directed along a linear path. Unforeseen consequences are inevitable.

6. Although you cannot direct outcomes, you can set up conditions that help to guide the process. "The challenge is to *disturb* them in a manner that approximates the desired outcomes" (Pascale, Millemann, and Gioja, 2000).

THE COMPLEXITIES OF LEADERSHIP

Leading in a culture of change entails unlocking the mysteries of living organizations, with emphasis placed on understanding and insight rather than on mere action steps. Complexities can be unlocked and even understood, but only rarely can they be controlled.

There are dilemmas in leading change. Goleman's analysis (2000) helps because it informs us that elements of different leadership styles must be learned and used in different situations. But if you are facing an urgent, crisis-ridden situation, a more coercive stance may be necessary at the beginning. Those dealing with failing enterprises have drawn this conclusion: the need for external intervention is in inverse proportion to how well the enterprise is progressing. In a case of persistent failure, dramatic, assertive leadership and external intervention appear to be necessary. In the long run, however, effectiveness depends on developing internal commitment in which the ideas and intrinsic motivation of the vast majority of organizational members become activated. Along the way, authoritative ideas, democratic empowerment, affiliative bonds, and coaching all are needed.

Previously we said that more coercive actions may be needed at the beginning of a crisis. This is where leadership becomes complicated. When an organization is in a crisis, it has to be rescued, so it needs authoritative leadership. But a crisis usually means that the organization is out of synch with its environment, which calls for accelerated change and learning. In this case, more radical change is required; the organization needs leadership that welcomes differences, communicates the urgency of the challenge, talks about broad possibilities in an inviting way, and creates mechanisms that "motivate people to reach beyond themselves" (Pascale, Millemann, and Gioja, 2000, p. 74; see also Heifetz, 1994).

There is a fine line between coercive and authoritative leadership. Recall the case example of the National Literacy and Numeracy Strategy in England. It has elements of coercive as well as pacesetting leadership. We don't really know whether this degree of pressure is required to get large-scale change under way, but we would venture to say that the strategy that moved the English school system from near chaos to a modicum of success is not the same strategy that is going to create the transformation needed for the system to thrive in the future. For that, it needs plenty of internal commitment and ingenuity.

The need to have different strategies for different circumstances explains why we cannot generalize from success stories. For example, of the forty-three excellent companies (and they were excellent at the time) featured in the book *In Search of Excellence* (Peters and Waterman, 1982), half were in trouble within five years of the book's appearance; by 2000, all but five had "fallen from grace" (Pascale, Millemann, and Gioja, 2000, p. 23).

To recommend employing different leadership strategies that simultaneously and sequentially combine different elements seems like complicated advice, but developing this deeper sense of the change process by accumulating insights and wisdom across situations and time may turn out to be the most practical thing we can do—more practical than the best step-by-step models. If such models don't work, or if they work only in some situations, or if they are successful only for short periods of time, they are hardly practical. We will review more about leadership behaviors in subsequent chapters.

Key Points About the Complexities of Leadership

1. Different leadership styles are effective in different situations.

2. In times of crisis or persistent failure, a more authoritative—even a coercive—stance may be necessary at the beginning. Dramatic, assertive leadership and external intervention may be necessary.

3. The paradox is that a crisis usually means that the organization is out of synch with its environment, which calls for accelerated change and learning. In this case, the organization needs leadership that welcomes differences, communicates the urgency of the challenge, talks about broad possibilities in an inviting way, and creates mechanisms that "motivate people to reach beyond themselves" (Pascale, Millemann, and Gioja, 2000, p. 74).

4. Decisive leaders can attract many followers, but it is usually more a case of dependence than enlightenment.

5. The strategy that moves a system from near chaos to a modicum of success is not the same strategy that will create the transformation needed for the system to thrive in the future. For that, plenty of internal commitment and ingenuity is needed.

6. In the long run, effectiveness depends on developing internal commitment in which the ideas and intrinsic motivation of the vast majority of organizational members become activated.

7. Along the way, authoritative ideas, democratic empowerment, affiliative bonds, and coaching are all needed.

The next stop in our practical journey is taking a new look at the importance of relationships in a culture of change.

Note your reactions to this chapter, any insights or questions it may have generated, or any specific things you might want to refer to later.

Key Points About Leadership Styles and Change

The six leadership styles that Goleman (2000) identified are:

1. Coercive: demands compliance. ("Do what I tell you.")
2. Authoritative: mobilizes people toward a vision. ("Come with me.")
3. Affiliative: creates harmony and builds emotional bonds. ("People come first.")
4. Democratic: forges consensus through participation. ("What do you think?")
5. Pacesetting: sets high standards for performance. ("Do as I do, now.")
6. Coaching: develops people for the future. ("Try this.")

 ## Lessons in Leadership Styles

1. Of the six leadership styles that Goleman (2000) identified, which two negatively affected climate and performance? Why?

2. Which of the leadership styles had a significant positive impact on climate and performance?

Leading in a Culture of Change: Personal Action Guide and Workbook

Key Points About the Change Process

- The goal is not to innovate the most.
- It is not enough to have the best ideas.
- Appreciate the implementation dip.
- Redefine resistance.
- Reculturing is the name of the game.
- Never a checklist, always complexity.

 ## Lessons About the Change Process

Lessons from "The Goal Is Not to Innovate the Most"

Write your answers to the questions that follow.

1. What are some of the drawbacks of pacesetter leadership?

2. What are some other things to be learned about change leadership in this section? (Although the sample answer quotes from the chapter, feel free to use your own words here.)

Lessons from "It Is Not Enough to Have the Best Ideas"

Write your answers to the questions that follow.

3. What are some of the drawbacks of coercive leadership?"

4. What are some other things to be learned about change leadership in this section? (Although the sample answer quotes from the chapter, feel free to use your own words here.)

Lessons from "Appreciate the Implementation Dip"

Write your answers to the questions that follow.

5. What is the implementation dip?

6. Why does the implementation dip occur?

7. How do pacesetting and coercive leaders respond to the implementation dip?

8. How do effective leaders view the implementation dip?

9. What types of leadership are needed during the implementation dip?

Lesson from "Redefine Resistance"

Write your answer to the question that follows.

10. What types of leaders are most effective in listening to resisters, and why is it important to listen to them?

Lesson from "Reculturing Is the Name of the Game"

Write your answer to the question that follows.

11. What is reculturing (what do you know so far about what it involves)?

Lesson from "Never a Checklist, Always Complexity"

Write your answers to the following.

12. Make some notes here on your basic understanding of complexity science.

Your Personal Assessment

Write your answers to the questions that follow.

1. How would you describe your own leadership style(s)?

2. When are these styles most effective in organizations?

3. What leadership styles might you need to develop in order to create a leadership repertoire that is equal to the challenges that organizations today are facing?

Things to Discuss with Others

Reality Check: Ask several persons whom you trust what they perceive your leadership style to be. Ask them when (that is, under what conditions) they think your style is most effective. If you trust them enough, ask them when they think your style is least effective. (Be aware that they may identify more than one style.) Write down here what they say.

What else have you learned in this chapter that you might discuss with specific others, to your developmental benefit?

 Things to Try Out

ANSWERS: Lessons in Leadership Styles

Of the six leadership styles identified by Goleman (2000), which two negatively affected climate and performance? Why? The coercive and pacesetting styles of leadership negatively affected climate and performance. People resent and resist the coercive style, and people become overwhelmed and burned out by the pacesetting style.

Which of the leadership styles had a significant positive impact on climate and performance? The authoritative, affiliative, democratic, and coaching styles had a significant positive impact on climate and performance.

ANSWERS: Lessons from "The Goal Is Not to Innovate the Most"

What are some of the drawbacks of pacesetter leadership?

Numerous superficial changes often lack depth and coherence. The pacesetter typically sets extremely high performance standards, and many employees feel overwhelmed by the continual demands to do things better and faster. Those who cannot are replaced. Morale and climate deteriorate. Pacesetters frequently do not attempt to build relationships with employees and other stakeholders.

What are some other things to be learned about change leadership in this section? Pacesetters must learn the difference between competing in a change marathon and developing the capacity and commitment to solve complex problems. It is important that a leader not assume that his or her version of what a change should be is one that should or could be implemented. No one can mandate what matters. Leaders can legislate reform but cannot mandate ownership and implementation. Any significant innovation, if it is to result in true change, requires individual implementers to work out their own meaning.

ANSWERS: Lessons from "It Is Not Enough to Have the Best Ideas"

What are some of the drawbacks of coercive leadership and so-called social engineering? A coercive leader may have some of the best ideas but not be able to get others to buy into them. Coercive leaders often experience overwhelming opposition. Although they may achieve short-term gains, morale deteriorates and productivity is negatively affected.

What are some other things to be learned about change leadership in this section? When there is an urgent problem and people are muddled, visionary leaders can be crucial. An authoritative leader with a clear vision can have a positive impact on climate and performance, exciting and mobilizing people to commit to the vision. Often, however, initial excitement cannot be sustained because it cannot be converted to internal commitment.

It is easy for authoritative leadership to slip into social engineering, which is based on mechanistic cause-and-effect thinking. Authoritative leaders need to recognize the weaknesses as well as the strengths in their approach. They need to use four or more of the successful leadership styles, especially the authoritative, democratic, affiliative, and coaching styles, to have the best climate and business performance (Goleman, 2000).

ANSWERS: Lessons from "Appreciate the Implementation Dip"

What is the implementation dip? The implementation dip is a dip in performance and confidence as one engages in an innovation that requires new skills and new understandings.

Why does the implementation dip occur? Innovations call on people to question and change their beliefs or behaviors (or both). When people who are used to knowing what they are doing are expected to learn new skills, they often feel anxious, fearful, confused, overwhelmed, deskilled, cautious, and even disturbed.

How do pacesetting and coercive leaders respond to the implementation dip? Pacesetters and coercers have no empathy for people who are undergoing implementation dips.

How do effective leaders view the implementation dip? Effective leaders know that change is a process. They understand when things don't go smoothly during the first year of a major change or new direction. They are empathic to the people immersed in the anxiety-ridden work of trying to bring about change. They know that these people are experiencing two kinds of problems: the social-psychological fear of change and the lack of technical know-how to make the change work.

What types of leadership are needed during the implementation dip? Leaders need affiliative and coaching styles during the implementation dip. The affiliative leader pays attention to people, focuses on building emotional bonds, builds relationships, and heals rifts. The coaching leader helps people to develop and invests in their capacity building (Goleman, 2000). Some elements of authoritative leadership also help: enthusiasm, self-confidence, optimism, and clarity of vision can inspire people. A problem arises when a leader is only authoritative, or only affiliative, or only a coach. Leaders who are sensitive to the implementation dip combine styles: they have an urgent sense of moral purpose and they measure success in terms of results, but they do things that are more likely to get the organization going and keep it going.

ANSWERS: Lesson from "Redefine Resistance"

What types of leaders are most effective in listening to resisters, and why is it important to do so? Leaders should seek out and listen to doubters (aspects of democratic leadership). They must try to build good relationships (be affiliative) even with those who may not trust them. Pacesetters and coercers are terrible listeners, and authoritative leaders are not good at listening either. Affiliative and democratic leaders may listen too much.

Resisters sometimes have ideas or see alternatives that the leader has missed, especially in situations of diversity or complexity or in looking for unknown answers. People resist for what they view as good reasons. They may understand problems about the minutiae of implementation that the leader does not (Maurer, 1996). Resisters are crucial when it comes to the politics of implementation. In democratic organizations, being alert to differences of opinion is vital. In all organizations, respecting resistance is essential; if leaders ignore it, it will take its toll during implementation, if not earlier. It is easy to sabotage implementation.

ANSWERS: Lesson from "Reculturing Is the Name of the Game"

What is reculturing (what do you know so far about what it involves)? Reculturing is creating a culture (not just a structure) of change. It activates and deepens moral purpose through collaborative work cultures that respect differences and continually create and test knowledge against measurable results. It creates the capacity to seek, critically assess, and selectively incorporate new ideas and practices both inside and outside the organization. It involves developing relationships, creating knowledge, and striving for coherence.

Building Relationships

*The role of the leader is to ensure
that the organization develops relationships
that help produce desirable results.*

Michael Fullan

If moral purpose is the first necessity, relationships are the second. In the past, if you asked someone in a successful enterprise what caused the success, the answer was, "It's the people." But that's only partially true; it is actually the *relationships* that make the difference. You can't get anywhere without them. The single factor common to every successful change initiative is that relationships improve. If relationships improve, things get better. If they remain the same or get worse, ground is lost. The combination of moral purpose and relational trust generates the wherewithal to go the extra mile.

Thus, leaders must be able to build relationships with and among diverse people and groups—especially with people different from themselves. Effective leaders know that people will be mobilized by caring and respect, by talented people working together, and by developing shared expertise.

RELATIONSHIPS IN BUSINESSES

In "Relationships: The New Bottom Line in Business," the first chapter of their book, *The Soul at Work,* Lewin and Regine (2000) talk about complexity science: "This new science, we found in our work, leads to a new theory of business that places people and relationships—how people interact with each other, the kinds of relationships they form—into dramatic relief. In a linear world, things may exist independently of each other, and when they interact, they do so in simple, predictable ways. In a nonlinear, dynamic world, everything exists only in relationship to everything else, and the interactions among agents in the system lead to complex, unpredictable outcomes. In this world, interactions, or relationships, among its agents are the organizing principle" (pp. 18–19).

To Lewin and Regine, "genuine relationships based on authenticity and care" are not just a product of networking. The "soul at work" is both individual and collective: "Actually, most people want to be part of their organization; they want to know the organization's purpose; they want to make a difference. When the individual soul is connected to the organization, people become connected to something deeper—the desire to contribute to a larger purpose, to feel they are part of a greater whole, a web of connection" (p. 27).

---

*"When the individual soul
is connected to the organization,
people become connected to something deeper."*

It is time, say Lewin and Regine, to alter our perspective: "to pay as much attention to how we treat people—co-workers, subordinates, customers—as we now typically pay attention to structures, strategies, and statistics" (p. 27). They say that there is a new style of leadership in successful companies, one that focuses on people and relationships as essential to getting sustained results:

> It's a new style in that it says, place more emphasis than you have previously on the micro level of things in your company, because this is a creative conduit for influencing many aspects of the macro level concerns, such as strategy and the economic bottom line. It's a new style

in that it encourages the emergence of a culture that is more open and caring. It's a new style in that it does not readily lend itself to being turned into "fix it" packages that are the stuff of much management consultancy, because it requires genuine connection with co-workers; you can't fake it and expect to get results [p. 57].

It is time to bury the cynic who said, "Leadership is about sincerity, and once you learn to fake that, you've got it made."

Lewin and Regine describe successful businesses that have a tough commitment to results supported by a deep regard for people inside and outside the organization. Examples range from Verifone, the electronic company that increased its revenues from $31.2 million to $600 million in eleven years, to Monsanto, the biotechnology company discussed in Chapter Two. Lewin and Regine cite Monsanto's main goal: to help people around the world "lead longer, healthier lives, at costs that they and their nation can afford, and without continued environmental degradation" (p. 208). Monsanto, using relationship and caring principles (as well as strategies for activating them), transformed itself from 1993 to 1999, quadrupling share prices. Lewin and Regine cite Monsanto's CEO, Shapiro, talking about Monsanto's awareness of human impact on the environment: "Around *that* coalesced a commitment to sustainable development, which you might describe as finding ways to continue economic growth while not negatively impacting the environment—even *improving* the environment, because that is going to be necessary" (p. 223).

Monsanto later faltered; although it was strongly connected inside, it failed to engage deeply enough with those on the outside. The lesson: never be complacent; reality-test your own rhetoric, assumptions, and plans with those (including skeptics and resisters) inside the organization and with people and groups outside the organization.

Kouzes and Posner (1998) discuss "encouraging the heart." They observe that "leaders create relationships" (p. xv) and identify seven essential components of creating relationships (p. 18):

1. Setting clear standards
2. Expecting the best
3. Paying attention
4. Personalizing recognition

5. Telling the story
6. Celebrating together
7. Setting the example

Kouzes and Posner conclude that what separates effective from ineffective leaders is how much they "really care about the people [they] lead" (p. 149). (Their twenty-one-item Encouragement Index is found on pages 36–37 of their book.)

Other business authors emphasize the importance of relationships. Dinkmeyer and Eckstein (1996) emphasize the importance of an encouraging leader and cite numerous examples from real businesses. Bishop (2000) argues that leadership in the twenty-first century must move from a product-first formula to a relationship-first formula. Goffee and Jones (2000) ask, "Why should anyone be led by you?" Their answer is that we should be led by leaders who inspire us by:

- Selectively showing their weaknesses (revealing humanity and vulnerability).

- Relying on intuition (interpreting emergent data).

- Managing with tough empathy (caring intensely about employees and about the work they do).

- Revealing their differences (showing what is unique about themselves). Collins (2001) found that leaders in "great" companies (those that had a sustained performance over fifteen years) had two main qualities: deep personal humility and intense professional will.

Key Points About Relationships

1. It's the interactions and relationships among people, not the people themselves, that make the difference in organizational success.

2. The factor common to every successful change initiative is that relationships improve. If relationships improve, things get better. If relationships remain the same or get worse, ground is lost.

3. Leaders must be able to build relationships with and among diverse people and groups, especially with people different from themselves.

4. Most people want to be part of their organization, to know the organization's purpose, and to make a difference or contribute to a larger purpose.

5. Leaders need to pay as much attention to how they treat people as they pay to structures, strategies, and statistics.

6. Successful businesses have a commitment to results supported by a deep regard for people inside and outside the organization.

7. Relationships with people and groups inside the organization (including skeptics and resisters) and outside the organization allow the leader and the organization to test their rhetoric, assumptions, and plans.

 ## Lessons About Leaders and Relationships

Write your answers to the questions that follow.

1. Think of a change initiative you know about in which attention was not paid to relationships. Can you attribute any problems or failures to the lack of good relationships among people or groups within the organization or to the organization's lack of relationships with key people outside it? Make some notes here.

2. What do Kouzes and Posner (1998) think separates effective from ineffective leaders?

3. Think back to the authentic leaders you listed at the beginning of Chapter Two. Can you see any of the characteristics described in this section in these leaders?

RELATIONSHIPS IN SCHOOLS

Let's look at a couple of examples in schools. First is the example of School District 2 in New York City. Elmore and Burney (1999, pp. 264–265) provide the context:

> District 2 is one of thirty-two community school districts in New York City. . . . District 2 has twenty-four elementary schools, seven junior high or intermediate schools, and seventeen. . . . Option Schools, which are alternative schools organized around themes with a variety of different grade configurations. District 2 has one of the most diverse student populations . . . in the city. It includes some of the highest-priced residential and commercial real estate in the world . . . and some of the most densely populated poorer communities in the city. . . . The student population . . . is twenty-two thousand, of whom about 29 percent are white, 14 percent black, about 22 percent Hispanic, 34 percent Asian, and less than 1 percent Native American.

Anthony Alvarado became superintendent of District 2 in 1987, when it ranked tenth in reading and fourth in mathematics out of thirty-two subdistricts. By 1996, it ranked second in both reading and mathematics. Elmore and Burney (1999) describe Alvarado's approach: "Over the eight years of Alvarado's tenure in District 2, the district has evolved a strategy for the use of professional development to improve teaching and learning in schools. This strategy consists of a set of organizing principles about the process of systemic change and the role of professional development in that process; and a set of specific activities, or models of staff development, that focus on systemwide improvement of instruction" (p. 266). The seven organizing principles of the reform strategy are as follows: (1) it's about instruction and only instruction; (2) instructional improvement is a long, multistage process involving awareness, planning, implementation, and reflection; (3) shared expertise is the driver of instructional change; (4) the focus is on systemwide improvement; (5) good ideas come from talented people working together; (6) set clear expectations, then decentralize; (7) collegiality, caring, and respect are paramount. Elmore and Burney (1999) explain:

> In District 2, professional development is a management strategy rather than a specialized administrative function. Professional development is what administrative leaders do when they are doing

their jobs, not a specialized function that some people in the organization do and others do not. Instructional improvement is the main purpose of district administration, and professional development is the chief means of achieving that purpose. Anyone with line administrative responsibility in the organization has responsibility for professional development as a central part of his or her job description. Anyone with staff responsibility has the responsibility to support those who are engaged in staff development. It is impossible to disentangle professional development from general management in District 2 because the two are synonymous for all practical purposes [p. 272].

Refer to the seven organizing principles from School District 2. In the space below, rewrite as many of these principles as possible so that they could apply to a change initiative in your team, department, or organization.

Another education example is described in a study by Newmann, King, and Youngs (2000) of what makes some schools especially effective. They conclude that what they call "school capacity" is the key to success. This capacity consists of five components: (1) teachers' knowledge, skills, and dispositions; (2) professional community; (3) program coherence; (4) technical resources; and (5) principal leadership. The role of these five components in combination is revealing and can apply to many organizations.

The knowledge, skills, and dispositions of teachers as *individuals* is obviously important and can make a difference in individual classrooms. However, Newmann, King, and Youngs assert that this is not sufficient, because the organization must change along with individuals. Professional development of individuals or even of small teams will not be sufficient. Schools must also focus on creating schoolwide *professional learning* communities.

Individual development combined with professional communities is still not sufficient unless it is channeled in a way that combats the fragmentation of multiple innovations; there must be *program coherence,* which Newmann, King, and Youngs (2000) define as "the extent to which the school's programs for student and staff learning are coordinated, focused on clear learning goals, and sustained over a period of time" (p. 5). Program coherence is organizational integration.

Another component of school capacity concerns the extent to which schools garner *technical resources.* Instructional improvement requires additional resources in the form of materials, equipment, space, time, and access to new ideas and expertise.

Schools are seriously undermined if they do not have *quality leadership.* The role of the principal is to "cause" the previous four factors to get better and better. Elmore (2000) agrees: "The job of administrative leaders is primarily about enhancing the skills and knowledge of people in the organization, creating a common culture of expectations around the use of those skills and knowledge, holding the various pieces of the organization together in a productive relationship with each other, and holding individuals accountable for their contributions to the collective result" (p. 15).

Development of individuals is not sufficient. New relationships (as found in a professional learning community) are crucial, but only if they work at the hard task of establishing greater program coherence and the addition of resources. The role of leadership is to "cause" greater capacity in the organization in order to get better results.

It is important to realize that relationships are not ends in themselves. Relationships are powerful, and they can be powerfully wrong. In a study of professional learning communities in sixteen high schools, McLaughlin and Talbert (2001) found only three schools with strong professional learning communities, and some departments within schools had strong communities while others had decidedly weak ones. In one school, for example, the English department had "the strongest technical culture of any department in our sample while the same school's social studies department ranks among the weakest" (p. 47).

Relationships are powerful,
and they can be powerfully wrong.

In the English department, "It's everyday practice that teachers are handing [out] sample lessons they've done, or an assignment that they've tried, and [discussing] when it worked [or] how they would do it differently. Or a new teacher joins the staff and instantly they are paired up with a couple of buddies . . . and file drawers and computer disks and everything are just made readily available" (p. 50). In contrast, teachers in the social studies department speak of "my materials" but never mention their colleagues as resources.

The teachers in the two departments demonstrate radically different assumptions about learning. English teachers' comments are uniformly positive: "We have excellent students, cooperative, and there's good rapport with the teachers." In contrast, a social studies teacher says of the same students, "There's no quest for knowledge. Not all, but that's in general . . . it's not important to them. They just don't want to learn."

McLaughlin and Talbert (2001) sum up the situation: "In the social studies department, autonomy means isolation and reinforces the norms of individualism and conservatism. In the English department, professional autonomy and strong community are mutually reinforcing, rather than oppositional. Here collegial support and interaction enable individual teachers to reconsider and revise their classroom practice confidently because department norms are mutually negotiated and understood" (p. 55).

McLaughlin and Talbert show the dramatically different effect these experiences have on the motivation and commitment of teachers: "English teachers of all pedagogical persuasions express pride in their department and pleasure in their work-place. . . . In contrast, social studies teachers, weary of grappling alone with class-room tensions, verbalize bitterness and professional disinvestment. Several plan to leave the school or the profession" (pp. 83–84).

As McLaughlin and Talbert (2001) point out, the effectiveness of strong pro-fessional communities depends on whether the members collaborate to make breakthroughs or whether they reinforce methods that do not achieve results. Weak collaboration is always ineffective, but strong communities can make matters worse if, in their collaboration, members reinforce one another's ineffective practices. Close relationships are not ends in themselves. Unless collaborative cultures are focusing on the right things, they may end up being powerfully wrong. Moral pur-pose, good ideas, focusing on results, and obtaining the views of dissenters are es-sential, because they mean that the organization is focusing on the right things.

The role of the leader is to ensure that the organization develops relationships that help produce desirable results. McLaughlin and Talbert (2001) conclude that leadership at the department or school level (or both) accounted for a large part of the difference in whether strong professional learning communities developed in a way that positively affected student learning:

> The English department chair actively maintained open department boundaries so that teachers would bring back knowledge resources from district and out-of-district professional activities to the commu-nity. English faculty attended state and national meetings, published regularly in professional journals, and used professional development days to visit classrooms in other schools. The chair gave priority for time to share each other's writing, discuss new projects, and just talk. . . . English department leadership extended and reinforced expecta-tions and opportunities for teacher learning provided by the district and by the school, developing a rich repertoire of resources for the community to learn.
>
> None of this applied down the hall in the social studies department, where leadership enforced the norms of privatism and conservatism that Dan Lortie [(1975) in his classic study of teachers] found central to school teaching. For example, the social studies chair saw depart-ment meetings as an irritating ritual rather than an opportunity: "I

don't hold meetings once a week; I don't even necessarily have them once a month." Supports or incentives for learning were few. . . . This department chair marginalized the weakest teachers in the department, rather than enabling or encouraging their professional growth [pp. 107–108].

In comparing effective professional learning communities with ineffective ones, McLaughlin and Talbert (2001) talk about the pivotal role of principal leadership:

The utter absence of principal leadership [in one school] . . . is a strong frame for the weak teacher community we found across departments in the school; conversely, strong leadership [in three other schools] has been central to engendering and sustaining these school-wide teacher learning communities. . . .

Principals with low scores [on leadership as perceived by teachers] generally are seen as managers who provide little support or direction for teaching and learning in the school. Principals receiving high ratings are actively involved in the sorts of activities that nurture and sustain strong teacher community [p. 110].

Briefly summarize what you have learned from the second case example about the two high school departments (for example, about building capacity, knowledge creation and sharing, and relationships in an organization).

Key Points from Second School Example

These points are from the study by Newmann, King, and Youngs of what makes schools effective.

1. Leaders must create professional learning communities that enhance the skills and knowledge of the people in the organization.

2. These learning communities must be channeled in a way that combats the fragmentation of multiple innovations; there must be program coherence.

3. There must be a common culture of expectations; individuals must be held accountable for their contributions to the collective result.

4. There must be ready access to technical resources, such as materials, equipment, space, time, and access to new ideas and expertise.

5. Strong communities can make matters worse if members reinforce ineffective practices.

6. Collegial communities are effective if members collaborate to share knowledge and make breakthroughs in learning.

7. The role of the leader is to ensure that the organization develops relationships that help produce desirable results.

 ## Lessons from School Examples

Write your answers to the questions that follow.

1. In the example of School District 2, what strategy was primarily used to improve teaching and learning in schools?

2. Think of an example, in an organization that you know about, of "fragmentation of multiple innovations" or lack of a "common culture of expectations" or reinforcement of ineffective practices. Make notes about what could have been done to avoid the condition.

3. What are some ways in which leaders in your organization could encourage development of a professional learning community? Write some specific examples (such as attending professional events or having members of a specific department visit other departments) and strategies for sharing the resulting knowledge.

LESSONS FOR BUSINESSES AND SCHOOLS

Not many businesses or schools operate in the manner espoused in this chapter. The cases presented are examples not of transformation but of preliminary steps. They reveals how deep the need for cultural change is. Part of cultural change is the understanding that successful strategies always involve relationships.

Where the world is heading (or needs to head) makes businesses and schools less different from each other than they have been in the past. The laws of nature and the new laws of sustainable human organizations are on the same evolutionary path. To be successful beyond the very short run, all organizations must incorporate moral purpose, understand complexity science, and respect, build, and draw on new human relationships with hitherto uninvolved constituencies inside and outside the organization. Doing these things is for their own good and the good of us all.

It would be a considerable understatement to say that leadership that combines all these elements is demanding. One very important thing in leading in a culture of change—which means helping people work together when anxiety and related emotions run high—is emotional intelligence.

EMOTIONAL INTELLIGENCE

Emotional intelligence concerns how leaders handle themselves and others in relation to the competencies described by Goleman, Boyatzis, and McKee (2002) and Stein and Book (2000). People have always needed emotional intelligence; in complex times, they need it more. The culture of change is rife with anxiety, stress, and ambiguity (and with the exhilaration of creative breakthroughs). It is not surprising that the most effective leaders are not those with the highest IQs but those who combine mental intelligence with emotional intelligence.

Effective leaders are not those with the highest IQs but those who combine mental intelligence with emotional intelligence.

Goleman (1995, 1998, 2000; Goleman, Boyatzis, and McKee, 2002) has done the seminal work on the topic of emotional intelligence. He and his colleagues cite countless examples and studies, such as the following (Goleman, 1998): "Claudio Ferández-Aráoz, in charge of executive searches throughout Latin America from Egon Zehnder International's Buenos Aires office, compared 227 highly successful executives with 23 who failed in their job. He found that the managers who failed were all high in expertise and IQ. In every case their fatal weakness was in emotional intelligence—arrogance, overreliance on brainpower, inability to adapt to the occasionally disorienting shifts in that region and disdain for collaboration or teamwork" (1998, p. 41). Goleman cites Kevin Murray, director of communications of British Airways: "Organizations going through the greatest change are those who need emotional intelligence the most" (p. 42).

Goleman, Boyatzis, and McKee (2002) identify four main sets of emotional competence (with several subdivisions), which they divide into the domains of personal and social competence:

Personal Competence

1. Self-awareness (knowing one's internal state, preferences, resources, and intuitions)

2. Self-management (managing one's internal states, impulses, and resources)

Social Competence

3. Social awareness (awareness of others' feelings, needs, and concerns)

4. Relationship management (developing a rapport with diverse others)

High emotional intelligence underpins the four leadership styles that Goleman (2000) found most effective in influencing culture and performance: authoritative, affiliative, democratic, and coaching. Low emotional intelligence is the hallmark of coercive and pacesetting leadership.

Stein and Book (2000) have taken these ideas further in developing the Emotional Quotient (EQ) inventory, which has been administered to more than forty-two thousand people. They say at the outset:

> Everyone knows people who could send an IQ test sky-high, but can't quite make good in either their personal or working lives. They rub others the wrong way; success just doesn't seem to pan out. Much of the time they can't figure out why. The reason why is that they're sorely lacking in emotional intelligence. . . .

In everyday language emotional intelligence is what we commonly refer to as "street smarts," or that uncommon ability we label "common sense." It has to do with the ability to read the political and social environment, and landscape them; to intuitively grasp what others want and need, what their strengths and weaknesses are; to remain unruffled by stress; and to be engaging, the kind of person that others want to be around [p. 14].

Stein and Book name five realms of EQ:

1. Intrapersonal (self-awareness, actualization, independence, and self-regard)
2. Interpersonal (empathy, social responsibility)
3. Adaptability (problem solving, flexibility)
4. Stress management (stress tolerance, impulse control)
5. General mood (happiness, optimism)

Stein and Book warn against the superficial use of EQ and recommend close examination of the strengths needed in certain jobs. For example, teachers need to be especially strong in optimism and stress management; those who are rigid and lacking in impulse control are ineffective. In working with ice hockey players, Stein and Book found that independence (a subdimension of EQ) had a reverse effect on sports success: talented players who went their own ways tended to underachieve.

In relationships, a high EQ is a must. The good news is that emotional intelligence can be learned; you can improve your EQ by working on it (Stein and Book, 2000; see also Chapter Seven). Effective leaders work on their own and others' emotional development. There is no greater skill needed for sustainable improvement.

Define emotional intelligence in your own words.

Key Points About Emotional Intelligence

1. The most effective leaders are those who combine mental intelligence with emotional intelligence.

2. Goleman, Boyatzis, and McKee (2002) identify four main sets of emotional competence:
   - Self-awareness (knowing one's internal state, preferences, resources, and intuitions)
   - Self-management (managing one's internal states, impulses, and resources)
   - Social awareness (awareness of others' feelings, needs, and concerns)
   - Relationship management (developing rapport with diverse others)

3. Stein and Book (2000) name five realms of emotional intelligence:
   - Intrapersonal (self-awareness, actualization, independence, and self-regard)
   - Interpersonal (empathy, social responsibility)
   - Adaptability (problem solving, flexibility)
   - Stress management (stress tolerance, impulse control)
   - General mood (happiness, optimism)

4. Emotional intelligence is displayed in the authoritative, affiliative, democratic, and coaching leadership styles.

5. Low emotional intelligence is displayed in coercive and pacesetting leadership.

RESISTANCE

In a culture of change, emotions frequently run high and often represent fear or differences of opinion. The nature of change includes fear of loss and obsolescence and feelings of awkwardness. People often express doubts about new directions and sometimes outright opposition to them.

The nature of change includes
fear of loss and obsolescence and
feelings of awkwardness.

Appreciating Resistance

Effective leaders in a culture of change appreciate resistance. They reframe it as having possible merit, and they almost always deal with it more effectively than anyone else. Dissent is seen as a potential source of new ideas and breakthroughs.

The absence of conflict can be a sign of decay. Pascale, Millemann, and Gioja (2000) note that prolonged "equilibrium is death" (p. 19). They use many examples to illustrate that allowing (even fostering) negative feedback is a step (not the only one) to needed improvement. One example is Jack Welch's "workout" at GE, in which "senior corporate officers were subjected to straight feedback from the troops in a series of public events. . . . Welch unleashed a process through which lower-level employees could shine the spotlight of public scrutiny on the most aggravating bureaucratic policies and redundant work practices" (p. 28). (Do not do this in your own organization unless you have all your EQ faculties intact and understand the entire process of acting on the results.)

Successful organizations in a culture of change have been found, to a certain extent, to seek diversity of employees, ideas, and experiences while simultaneously establishing mechanisms for sorting out, reconciling, and acting on new patterns (see Lewin and Regine, 2000, and Pascale, Millemann, and Gioja, 2000). Diverse people within a system can provide valuable information about how things work now, the impacts that particular changes might have, and the amount of support or resistance that is likely to be encountered in a specific area. Investing only in like-minded innovators is not necessarily a good thing. They become more like-minded and more unlike the rest of the organization while missing valuable new clues about the future. By supporting the like-minded, leaders trade off early smoothness for later grief. If you include and value naysayers, noise in the early stages will yield later, greater implementation. Listen to Heifetz's seemingly counterintuitive advice, "Respect those you wish to silence" (1994, p. 271), and Maurer's touchstones for "getting beyond the wall of resistance" (1996, p. 54), which include maintaining a clear focus while you take the concerns of resisters seriously. As he points out, the only way to deal with resistance is to work with resisters.

*Not all groups within the system
will view the same things in the same ways.*

Working with Resistance

Effective change leaders acknowledge the uncertainty, anxiety, and disagreement in the system, at the individual level, team level, and higher levels. They know that not all groups within the system will view the same things in the same ways. They don't expect everyone to internalize the vision at the beginning and they know they need to build ownership through doing. They also know that resisters often can tell them what's wrong. Effective leaders access the collective intelligence of the system by listening to diverse people and groups, including questioners and resisters. They acknowledge others' concerns, use their insights, and invite them to participate in informed discussion and exploration. Overall, they work with resistance by doing the following:

1. Knowing that anxiety, fear, and resistance are natural effects of change and educating people within the system about this tendency

2. Soliciting and listening to the concerns and ideas of people and groups whose lives are going to be changed

3. Identifying the concerns and ideas of various groups within the system

4. Acknowledging the overload, fragmentation, and other stresses that can accompany change initiatives

5. Addressing these concerns and ideas in public statements

6. Incorporating these concerns and ideas into the ongoing dialogue about change

7. Exploring resisters' intentions

8. Knowing and identifying self-imposed barriers to change (for example, perceived limitations, role ambiguity, if-only thinking, lack of responsibility, not taking charge of one's own learning and development) and helping people to overcome them

9. Creating the expectation that change is a given, so directing it is a good thing

10. Validating positive risk taking and exploration

11. Enlisting the support of middle managers in working with diverse groups

12. Reducing fragmentation by helping diverse groups to explore and overcome their differences (for example, by establishing lines of communication and information sharing and by providing skilled mediation)

13. Checking the accuracy of data and interpretations that accompany the change effort

14. Identifying options and working to find common ground

15. Refraining from initiating too many innovations that aren't connected at one time

The more that leaders do the above, the more they are in a position to take decisive action when necessary, including removing ineffective and uncaring employees.

Key Points About Appreciating and Working with Resistance

1. The nature of change includes fear of loss and obsolescence and feelings of awkwardness.

2. Effective change leaders acknowledge the uncertainty, anxiety, and resistance that accompany change and they educate people within the system about these tendencies.

3. Effective change leaders help people to identify self-imposed barriers to change.

4. Effective change leaders solicit and listen to the concerns and ideas of people and groups whose lives are going to be changed. They check the accuracy of data and interpretations.

5. Resistance is a potential source of new information, ideas, and breakthroughs. Like-minded innovators may miss valuable clues about the future.

6. Equilibrium, that is, the absence of conflict, can be a sign of system decay.

7. Successful organizations seek diversity of employees, ideas, and experiences while establishing mechanisms for sorting out, reconciling, and acting on new patterns.

8. Effective leaders create the expectation that change is a given, so directing it is a good thing. They validate positive risk taking and exploration.

9. Effective change leaders reduce fragmentation by helping diverse groups to explore and overcome their differences. They help to identify options and work to find common ground.

10. Effective change leaders do not initiate too many innovations that aren't connected at one time.

11. Effective leaders do take action against persistently poorly performing and uncaring individuals, but they do this in the light of the previous ten points.

Building Relational Trust

In the case example of high schools by McLaughlin and Talbert (2001), one of the obvious results of collegial sharing and development in the English department (which likely did not occur in the social studies department) was trust among the members of the department. As Bryk and Schneider (2002) point out, relational trust is "forged in daily social exchanges—trust grows over time through exchanges where the expectations held for others are validated in action" (pp. 136–137). Relational trust erodes when people perceive that others are not acting in ways that are consistent with the understandings of the others' role obligations: "Relational trust facilitates the development of beliefs, values, organizational routines, and individual behaviors that instrumentally affect . . . engagement and learning" (p. 115). It also "facilitates public problem solving" and "creates a moral resource" for improvement (pp. 116–117).

According to Bryk and Schneider, relational trust includes competence, respect, personal regard for others, and integrity. Effective leaders know how to build the trust necessary for effective change through healthy relationships between, and ongoing development of, all members and levels of the organization (Fullan, 2003b). The interaction and collaboration of working together in a new endeavor with moral purpose help to diffuse the tension and anxiety in the system—especially in people who might have started off thinking that change was being imposed on them without their having any part in directing it.

Effective leaders know how to build the trust necessary for effective change.

Bryk and Schneider (2002) also found that high-trust cultures produce some of the specific organizational features that are essential for working through complex, demanding change processes: they (1) enable risk and effort; (2) facilitate problem solving; (3) coordinate clear, collective action; and (4) sustain ethical and moral imperative.

In *Trust and Betrayal in the Workplace,* Reina and Reina (1999) identify three types of trust, all of which must be actively developed and reinforced:

1. Competence Trust (trust of capability)

   - Respect people's knowledge, skills, and abilities.

   - Respect people's judgment.

   - Involve others and seek their input.

   - Help people learn skills.

2. Contractual Trust (trust of character)

   - Manage expectations.

   - Establish boundaries.

   - Delegate appropriately.

   - Encourage mutually serving intentions.

   - Honor agreements.

   - Be consistent.

3. Communications Trust (trust of disclosure)

   - Share information.

   - Tell the truth.

- Admit mistakes.

- Give and receive constructive feedback.

- Maintain confidentiality.

- Speak with good purpose.

In summary, providing developmental opportunities and creating environments in which people are encouraged to learn, interact, share, take risks, and tackle problems all help to create trust.

 ### Lessons About Building Trust

Write your answers to the items that follow.

1. In your own words, describe what *creates* relational trust in any organization.

2. List some key elements of such trust.

Key Points About Building Trust

Reina and Reina (1999) identify three types of trust, all of which must be actively developed and reinforced:

1. Competence Trust (trust of capability)

   • Respect people's knowledge, skills, and abilities.

   • Respect people's judgment.

   • Involve others and seek their input.

   • Help people learn skills.

2. Contractual Trust (trust of character)

   • Manage expectations.

   • Establish boundaries.

   • Delegate appropriately.

   • Encourage mutually serving intentions.

   • Honor agreements.

   • Be consistent.

3. Communications Trust (trust of disclosure)

   • Share information.

   • Tell the truth.

   • Admit mistakes.

   • Give and receive constructive feedback.

   • Maintain confidentiality.

   • Speak with good purpose.

We know that the development of relationships among diverse elements in the organization, including those who raise objections, is essential. The next stop on our journey concerns the role of knowledge, another convergence. Sharing knowledge fuels relationships.

Note your reactions to this chapter, any insights or questions it may have generated, or any specific things you might want to refer to later.

Your Personal Assessment

Goffee and Jones (2000) say that leaders inspire us by

- Selectively showing their weaknesses (revealing humanity and vulnerability)

- Relying on intuition (interpreting emergent data)

- Managing with tough empathy (caring intensely about employees and about the work they do)

- Revealing their differences (showing what is unique about themselves)

Write your answers to the questions that follow.

1. How often do you think you display each of these behaviors? Why do you or why do you not?

2. What do you need to work on in terms of your own capacities as a leader in regard to these behaviors?

3. Identify a time when you showed emotional intelligence in dealing with a person or situation. Then identify a time when you did *not,* and describe how you might have handled the situation differently.

4. How do you think others perceive you in terms of emotional intelligence? Does this differ in your private life and your work life? If so, how?

5. What do you need to work on in terms of your own capacities as a leader in regard to emotional intelligence?

6. What are your typical feelings when faced with imminent change or the likelihood of change that you did not willingly initiate? Use "emotion" words (such as *fear, anxiety, excitement*) to describe your feelings.

7. What is your typical response to such change (that is, how do you behave)? How do your feelings affect your behavior?

8. How might this insight help you to better empathize with others within an organization who are faced with change that they did not initiate?

9. How have you dealt with resistance to change within your team, department, or organization in the past? What would you do differently now?

10. What do you need to work on in terms of your own capacities as a leader, in regard to appreciating and working with resistance, developing trust, and so on?

Things to Discuss with Others

Talking about these issues with others helps you to widen the lens. What have you learned in this chapter that you might discuss with specific others, to your developmental benefit?

Things To Try Out

The next time you encounter resistance, make a point of sitting down with the resister and obtaining information about the divergent points of view. Practice your skills in acknowledging and working with the resistance.

Other Things to Try Out

ANSWERS: Lessons About Leaders and Relationships

What do Kouzes and Posner (1998) think separates effective from ineffective leaders?

Kouzes and Posner conclude that what separates effective from ineffective leaders is how much they "really care about the people they lead."

ANSWERS: Lesson from School Examples

In the first case example (School District 2), what strategy was primarily used to improve teaching and learning in schools?

Professional development was the strategy used in District 2 to improve teaching and learning in schools.

Creating and Sharing Knowledge

*All organizations would be better off if they strengthened their capacity
to access and leverage hidden knowledge.*

Michael Fullan

Knowledge creation, knowledge building, knowledge sharing, knowledge management: these could easily become just buzzwords unless we understand the role of knowledge in organizational performance and set up the mechanisms and practices that make knowledge creation and sharing a cultural value.

KNOWLEDGE IS A SOCIAL PHENOMENON

Information is on paper and in computers. Knowledge is in people. The technocrats are wrong in thinking that if only we can provide greater access to more information for more people, we will have it made. Data without relationships merely increase the information glut. Brown and Duguid (2000) establish the foundation for viewing knowledge as a social phenomenon:

Attending too closely to information overlooks the social context that helps people understand what that information might mean and why it matters [p. 5].

For all information's independence and extent, it is people, in their communities, organizations, and institutions, who ultimately decide what it all means and why it matters [p. 18].

A viable system must embrace not just the technological system, but the social system—the people, organizations, and institutions involved [p. 60].

Knowledge is something we digest rather than merely hold. It entails the knower's understanding and some degree of commitment [p. 120].

Envisioned change will not happen or will not be fruitful until people look beyond the simplicities of information and individuals to the complexities of learning, knowledge, judgment, communities, organizations, and institutions [p. 213].

Leading in a culture of change does not mean placing changed individuals into unchanged environments. This is why sending individuals or teams to external training does not work by itself: because it focuses on information rather than its use.

Think about the following statements: "Information is not pertinent until people decide what it means and why it matters." "It is a mistake to focus on information rather than its use." Have you thought about information in this way before? Rewrite the principle that information is relevant only in terms of its use in your own words.

Most organizations have invested heavily in technology (and possibly training) but scarcely in knowledge creation and sharing. When they do attempt to share and use new knowledge, they find it enormously difficult. Take the seemingly obvious notion of sharing best practices within an organization. Identifying the practices usually goes reasonably well, but when it comes to transferring and using the knowledge, the organization often flounders. For example, Hewlett-Packard attempted "to raise quality levels around the globe by identifying and circulating the best practices within the firm" (Brown and Duguid, 2000); the effort became so frustrating that it prompted Lew Platt, chairman of HP, to wryly observe, "If only we knew what we know at HP" (p. 123).

Accessing Tacit Knowledge

In their study of successful Japanese companies, Nonaka and Takeuchi (1995) explain that the companies were successful not because of their use of technology but because of their expertise at creating organizational knowledge, which the authors define as "the capability of a company as a whole to create new knowledge, disseminate it throughout the organization, and embody it in products, services and systems" (p. 3). Building on earlier work by Polyani (1983), Nonaka and Takeuchi make the crucial distinction between *explicit* knowledge (words and numbers that can be communicated in the form of data and information) and *tacit* knowledge (skills, beliefs, and understanding that are below the level of awareness):

> [Japanese companies] recognize that the knowledge expressed in words and numbers represents only the tip of the iceberg. They view knowledge as being primarily "tacit"—something not easily visible and expressible. Tacit knowledge is highly personal and hard to formalize, making it difficult to communicate or share with others. Subjective insights, intuitions, and hunches fall into this category of knowledge. Furthermore, tacit knowledge is deeply rooted in an individual's action and experience, as well as in the ideals, values, or emotions that he or she embraces [p. 8].

Successful organizations access tacit knowledge. Nonaka and Takeuchi (1995) say, "The sharing of tacit knowledge among multiple individuals with different backgrounds, perspectives, and motivations becomes the critical step for organizational knowledge creation to take place. The individuals' emotions, feelings, and mental models have to be shared to build mutual trust" (p. 85). Success is found in the intricate relationships and interaction inside and outside the organization that converts tacit knowledge to explicit knowledge on an ongoing basis.

Accessing tacit knowledge is not an easy process. First, tacit knowledge is, by definition, hard to get at. Individuals who work alone are subject to feelings of isolation and limits to growth, so they may hoard their knowledge. When work groups do not interact with others, the members become loyal to the group rather than to the organization. People do not voluntarily share knowledge unless the culture favors exchange (there is a moral commitment to share or rewards for doing so, or both). Second, the process must sort out and yield quality ideas; not all tacit knowledge is useful. Third, quality ideas must be retained, shared, and used throughout the organization.

People do not voluntarily share knowledge unless the culture favors exchange.

Von Krogh, Ichijo, and Nonaka (2000) subtitled their book, *How to Unlock the Mystery of Tacit Knowledge and Release the Power of Innovation*. Lamenting the overuse of information technology, they explain how effective companies combine care or moral purpose with an understanding of the change process and an emphasis on developing relationships (corresponding to Chapters Two through Four in this book): "Knowledge enabling includes facilitating relationships and conversations as well as sharing local knowledge across an organization or beyond geographic and cultural borders. At a deeper level, however, it relies on a new sense of emotional knowledge and care in the organization, one that highlights how people treat each other and encourages creativity" (p. 4).

Creating a Culture of Sharing

Malcolm Gladwell (2000) says, "Behavior is a function of social context" (p. 150). This means that environment shapes behavior (for example, people tend to behave more politely in certain environments than in others). The context is social, not individual. The idea is to "create a community around them, where these new beliefs could be practical, expressed and nurtured" (p. 173). Knowledge, as distinct from information, "is closely attached to human emotions, aspirations, hopes, and intention" (Von Krogh, Ichijo, and Nonaka, 2000, p. 30). In other words, there is an explicit and intimate link between sharing knowledge and internal commitment on the way to making good things happen (the results part of Figure 1.1).

Kotter and Cohen (2002) say, "People rarely change through a rational process of analyze-think-change" (p. 11). They are much more likely to change in a see-feel-change sequence. The role of the leader is to help create a process that helps people see new possibilities that engage their emotions and thus change behaviors or reinforce changed behavior. This is why effective change leaders work on changing the context, helping to create new settings that are conducive to learning and to sharing the learning.

Effective change leaders work on changing the context.

Let's look at the conditions under which people share knowledge. Von Krogh, Ichijo, and Nonaka (2000) elaborate:

> Knowledge creation puts particular demands on organizational relationships. In order to share personal knowledge, individuals must rely on others to listen and react to their ideas. Constructive and helpful relations enable people to share their insights and freely discuss their concerns. They also enable microcommunities, the origin of knowledge creation in companies, to form and self-organize. Good relationships purge a knowledge-creation process of distrust, fear, and dissatisfaction, and allow organizational members to feel safe enough to explore the unknown territories of new markets, new customers, new products, and new manufacturing technologies [p. 45].

Changing the context means changing the conditions under which people operate. This includes naming knowledge sharing as a value, creating mechanisms to enable it, and reinforcing it when it occurs. Here are some ways to create the conditions and processes that enhance the likelihood of greater ownership and commitment (Fullan, 2003a):

1. Start with moral purpose, key problems, and desirable directions—but don't lock in; allow room for exploration and contribution.
2. Create communities of interaction around these ideas.
3. Ensure that quality information infuses interaction and related deliberations.
4. Look for promising patterns; consolidate gains and build on them.

In collaborative cultures, sharing and support create trust, feelings of collegiality and professionalism, greater capability, and continual improvement (Fullan, 2003b). This chapter contains several examples of knowledge creation and sharing. Organizations that do this well are still in the minority, but they are the wave of the future. What we can learn from them dovetails perfectly with the discussions in previous chapters.

---

*In collaborative cultures,
sharing and support create trust.*

Key Points About Knowledge Is a Social Phenomenon

1. Information is not pertinent until people decide what it means and why it matters.

2. It is a mistake to focus on information rather than its use.

3. A successful organization creates organizational knowledge, disseminates it throughout the organization, and embodies it in products, services, and systems.

4. Explicit knowledge exists as data and information. Tacit knowledge exists as the skills, beliefs, insights, and understandings within individuals.

5. A successful organization accesses tacit knowledge inside and outside the organization and converts it to explicit knowledge on an ongoing basis.

6. Environment shapes behavior. People do not voluntarily share knowledge unless the culture favors exchange (there is a moral commitment to share).

7. Not all tacit knowledge is useful; the organization must sort out and identify quality ideas and then share and use them throughout the organization.

8. People are more likely to change through a process of see-feel-change than through a process of analyze-think-change. The role of the leader is to create a process that helps people see new possibilities that engage their emotions and thus change behaviors or reinforce changed behavior.

9. Individuals must believe that others will listen to their ideas and allow them to discuss their concerns before they will be willing to share personal knowledge. When sharing is a cultural value and is rewarded, the process is purged of distrust and fear, and organizational members feel safe enough to explore possibilities together.

10. Effective change leaders work on changing the context, helping to create new settings that are conducive to learning and to sharing the learning (naming

knowledge sharing as a value, creating mechanisms to enable it, and reinforcing it when it occurs). Changing the context means changing the conditions under which people operate. This includes naming knowledge sharing as a value, creating mechanisms to enable it, and reinforcing it when it occurs.

11. Some ways to create the conditions and processes that enhance the likelihood of greater ownership and commitment are:

- Start with moral purpose, key problems, and desirable directions—but don't lock in; allow room for exploration and contribution.
- Create communities of interaction around these ideas.
- Ensure that quality information infuses interaction and related deliberations.
- Look for promising patterns; consolidate gains and build on them.

12. In collaborative cultures, the context is social, not individual. Sharing and support create trust, feelings of collegiality and professionalism, greater capability, and continual improvement.

EXAMPLES FROM BUSINESS

Von Krogh, Ichijo, and Nonaka (2000) emphasize that a culture of care is vital for successful performance, which they define in five dimensions:

1. Mutual trust
2. Active empathy
3. Access to help
4. Lenience in judgment
5. Courage

When you see the U.S. Army, British Petroleum, Gemini Consulting, KPMG, Monsanto, Sears, and a host of other companies in "tough" businesses espousing quality relationships as vital to their success, you know there's something to it.

Many of us have experienced the consequences of not attending to these matters. Von Krogh, Ichijo, and Nonaka (2000) summarize Darrah's study (1993) of a computer components supplier:

The company faced severe productivity and quality problems. Management's response was to punish ignorance and lack of expertise among factory-floor workers; at the same time, whenever they ran into manufacturing problems, it explicitly discouraged them from seeking help from the engineers who designed the components and organized the production line. These workers gained individual knowledge through seizing: They worked on sequentially defined manufacturing tasks and tried to come to terms with the task at hand, without thinking through the consequences for the performance of other tasks at other stages of the manufacturing process. When a new worker was employed, he received little training. Yet for productivity and cost reasons, the novice would be put to work as soon as possible. Knowledge transactions between workers and engineers were very rare, and most of the knowledge on the factory floor remained tacit and individual. The tacit quality of individual knowledge was pushed even farther because the foremen would not allow personal notes or drawings to help solve tasks.

Concerned with the severe productivity and quality problems, a new production director suggested a training program for factory workers that would help to remedy the situation. The program was designed in a traditional teaching manner: The product and manufacturing engineers were supposed to explain the product design and give an overall view of the manufacturing process and requirements for each step. At the end of the training session, the engineers would ask the workers for their opinions and constructive input—knowledge transaction intended to improve quality and communication. The workers, however, knew the consequences of expressing ignorance and incompetence, and they did not discuss the problems they experienced, even if they knew those problems resulted from flaws in product design. Nor did they have a legitimate language in which to express their concerns and argue "on the same level" as the engineers. The workers mostly remained silent, the training program did not have the desired effects, and the director left the company shortly thereafter [pp. 56–57].

Knowledge Sharing Creates a Collaborative Culture

Most people assume that there is a causal relationship between good relationships and knowledge sharing: you build relationships first and then information will flow. Von Krogh, Ichijo, and Nonaka (2000) seem to accept this view: "We believe a broad acceptance of the emotional lives of others is crucial for establishing good working relationships—and good relations, in turn, lead to effective knowledge creation" (p. 51).

We tend, however, to agree with Dixon (2000). One myth, observes Dixon, is that

the exchange of knowledge happens only in organizations that have a noncompetitive or a collaborative culture. It follows that the first thing you have to do is to fix the culture and then get people to share. But I have found that it's the other way around. If people begin sharing ideas about issues they see as really important, the sharing itself creates a learning culture. I have, of course, inserted an important caveat in that sentence: "about issues they see as really important."

Ford supplies an illustration of this point. Every Ford plant is responsible for making a 5 percent productivity increase every year. People in the plant refer to it as the "task." This is serious business; as one plant manager said, "If you don't make your task, your successor will." Year after year it is a real chore to keep making the 5 percent task, as production engineers are stretched to find some new process or technique to reduce the cost of labor, materials, or energy. Now, the Best Practice Replication process sends the production engineer in each Vehicle Operations plant five to eight best practices items a week, each of which describes how a sister plant reduced costs. Each item spells out exactly how much was saved, specified in hours, materials, or energy. The production engineers have come to rely on this system as a way to make their task. In fact, on average, 40 percent of task comes from best practices pulled off the system—and in some plants 100 percent of task is taken from the system. It is significant that this system is so well used in an industry that is known for being highly competitive. People use it because the system offers help with a very critical business need. But what has also happened at Ford as a result of this ongoing exchange is a change in the company's culture. A learning culture is developing based on this experiential understanding of why knowledge sharing is important.

It is a kind of chicken-or-egg issue: Which comes first, the learning culture or the exchange of knowledge? Given many organizations' rather abysmal success rate at changing their culture, I would put my money on having the exchange impact the culture rather than waiting for the culture to change [pp. 5–6].

Have you thought about knowledge sharing as a medium for creating a collaborative culture? What is your response to this insight?

In other words, establishing knowledge-sharing practices is as much a route to creating collaborative cultures as it is a product of them. This means that the organization must frame the giving and receiving of knowledge as a responsibility and must reinforce such sharing through incentives and opportunities to engage in it.

The organization must frame the giving and receiving of knowledge as a responsibility.

Von Krogh, Ichijo, and Nonaka (2000) draw the same conclusion when they talk about two interrelated responsibilities: "From our standpoint, a 'caring expert' is an organizational member who reaches her level of personal mastery in tacit and explicit knowledge *and* understands that she is responsible for sharing the process" (p. 52).

The Elements of Knowledge Exchange

Figure 5.1 illustrates the elements of knowledge exchange. Knowledge is continually given and received, as organizations provide opportunities to do so and value and reward individuals who do. The logic of this should be clear:

- Complex, turbulent environments constantly generate messiness and reams of ideas.

- Interacting individuals are the key to accessing and sorting out these ideas.

- Individuals will not engage in sharing unless they find it motivating to do so—whether because they feel valued and are valued, because they are getting something in return, or because they want to contribute to a bigger vision.

Figure 5.1. Knowledge-Sharing Paradigm

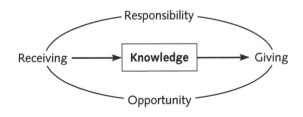

Effective leaders in a culture of change realize that accessing tacit knowledge is crucial and that such access cannot be mandated. They understand the value and role of knowledge creation, and they make it a priority, establishing and reinforcing habits of knowledge exchange among organizational members. To do this, they must create many mechanisms by which people can engage in this new behavior and learn to value it. Control freaks need not apply; people need elbow room to uncover and sort out best ideas. Leaders must learn to trust the processes they set up, look for promising patterns, and continually refine and identify procedures for maximizing valuable sharing. Knowledge activation, as Von Krogh, Ichijo, and Nonaka (2000) call it, "is about enabling, not controlling. . . . Anyone who wants to be a knowledge activist must give up, at the outset, the idea of controlling knowledge creation" (p. 158). They elaborate: "From an enabling perspective, knowledge that is transferred from other parts of the company should be thought of as a source of inspiration and insights for a local business operation, not a direct order that must be followed. Control of knowledge is local, tied to local re-creation. . . . The local unit uses the received knowledge as input to spark its own continuing knowledge-creation process" (p. 213).

Accessing tacit knowledge is crucial.

It is important to note that companies must name knowledge sharing as a core value and then establish mechanisms and procedures that embody the value in action. Dixon (2000) provides several illustrations:

> One of the best examples . . . is British Petroleum's Peer Assist Program. Peer Assist enables a team that is working on a project to call upon another team (or a group of individuals) that has had experience in the same type of task. The teams meet face-to-face for one to three days in order to work through an issue the first team is facing. For example, a team that is drilling in deep water off the coast of Norway can ask for an "assist" from a team that has had experience in deep-water drilling in the gulf of Mexico. As the label implies, "assists" are held between peers, not with supervisors or corporate "helpers." The idea of Peer Assists was put forward by a corporate task force in late 1994, and

BP wisely chose to offer it as a simple idea without specifying rules or lengthy "how-to" steps. It is left up to the team asking for the assistance to specify who it would like to work with, what it wants help on, and at what stage in the project it could use the help. . . .

Probably the best-known example of leveraging knowledge within a team is the U.S. Army's use of After Action Reviews. The AARs are held at the end of any team or unit action with the intent of reusing what has been learned immediately in the next battle or project. These brief meetings are attended by everyone who was engaged in the effort, regardless of rank. The Army's simple guidelines for conducting AARs are (1) no sugar coating, (2) discover ground truth, (3) no thin skins, (4) take notes, and (5) call it like you see it. The meetings are facilitated by someone in the unit, sometimes the ranking officer but just as often another member of the team. The learning from these meetings is captured both by the members, who all write and keep personal notes about what they need to do differently, and by the facilitator, who captures on a flip chart or chalkboard what the unit as a whole determines that it needs to do differently in the next engagement. Army After Action Reviews have standardized three key questions: What was supposed to happen? What happened? And what accounts for the difference? An AAR may last fifteen minutes or an hour depending on the action that is being discussed, but in any case, it is not a lengthy meeting. . . .

Bechtel's Steam Generator Replacement Group also uses this practice, although it calls the meetings "lessons learned" instead of AARs. Bechtel is a multibillion-dollar international engineering, procurement, and construction company engaged in large-scale projects, such as power plants, petrochemical facilities, airports, mining facilities, and major infrastructure projects. Unlike other parts of Bechtel in which individuals work in ever-changing project teams, the Steam Generator Replacement Group is a small specialized unit that works on a lot of jobs together. Anything learned on one job can be immediately used by the team on the next job. The nature of its work leaves little room for error. The average window of time to replace a steam generator is seventy days or less, unlike the typical Bechtel project, which may last two years or more. This unforgiving schedule mandates that the Steam Generator Replacement Group learn from its own lessons, because even a small mistake can result in a significant delay to a project. The lessons are captured in two ways: first, in weekly meetings to which supervisors are required to bring lessons learned; then, at the end of each project, the project manager brings all players together for a full day to focus on the lessons learned [pp. 9, 37–40].

The design criteria underlying these examples are crucial: (1) they focus on the intended users; (2) they are parsimonious (no lengthy written statements or meetings); (3) they try to get at tacit knowledge (this is why personal interaction or exchange is key and why dissemination of "products" or explicit knowledge by itself is rarely sufficient); (4) learning takes place in context with other members of the organization; and (5) they do not aim for faithful replication or control.

Accessing and creating new knowledge from the outside is more complicated.

We could do well enough if we harnessed intracompany knowledge. Accessing and creating new knowledge from the outside is more complicated (see the examples in Pascale, Millemann, and Gioja, 2000). Whether one is promoting intracompany exchanges or accessing external knowledge, the principles are the same: make knowledge building a core value and create specific opportunities to engage in the process. If Shell can do it with 105,000 employees dispersed among 130 operating companies, we all can do it. In all these cases, there is a need to establish specific procedures and opportunities, such as the "fishbowl" at Shell, described by Steven Miller, the managing director of the new Oil Products Business Committee (quoted in Pascale, Millemann, and Gioja, 2000):

One of the most important innovations in changing all of us was the fishbowl. The name describes what it is: I and a number of my management team sit in the middle of a room with one of the country teams in the center with us. The other team members listen from the outer circle. Everyone is watching as the group in the hot seat talks about what they're going to do, and what they need from me and my colleagues to be able to do it. That may not sound revolutionary—but in our culture it was very unusual for anyone lower in the organization to talk this directly to a managing director and his reports.

In the fishbowl, the pressure is on to measure up. . . . If a team brings in a plan that's really a bunch of crap, we've got to be able to call it a bunch of crap. If we cover for people or praise everyone, what do we say when someone brings in an excellent plan? That kind of straight talk is another big culture change for Shell.

The whole process creates complete transparency between the people at the coal face and me and my top management team. At the end, these folks go back home and say, "I just cut a deal with the managing director and his team to do these things." It creates a personal connection—and it changes how we talk with each other and how we work with each other. The country leaders go along because it provides support for what needed to be done anyway. After that, I can call up those folks anywhere in the world and talk in a very direct way because of this personal connectedness. It has completely changed the dynamics of our operations [pp. 188–189].

The fishbowls, note Pascale, Millemann, and Gioja (2000), are staged for dramatic effect to accomplish work and generate commitment: "The proceedings are videotaped so that when teams return to their operating companies, stakeholders from middle and upper management who were not present at the workshop can watch and learn from the visual record. (These inexpensive videos had a huge multiplier effect on the transformation of Shell's Downstream business)" (p. 224).

In the same vein, Garvin (2000), after examining several case examples of knowledge-building organizations, summarizes the role of leaders: "First, leaders and managers must create opportunities for learning by designing settings and events that prompt the necessary activities. Second, they must cultivate the proper tone, fostering desirable norms, behaviors, and rules of engagement. Third, they must personally lead the process of discussion, framing debate, posing questions, listening attentively, and providing feedback and closure" (pp. 190–191).

"Leaders and managers must create opportunities for learning."

Key Points from Business Examples

1. Von Krogh, Ichijo, and Nonaka (2000) define the elements of a culture of care, which is vital for successful performance: mutual trust, active empathy, access to help, lenience in judgment, and courage.

2. Establishing interactive knowledge-sharing practices is as much a route to creating collaborative cultures as it is a product of them.

3. An organization must frame the giving and receiving of knowledge as a responsibility and must reinforce such sharing through incentives and opportunities to engage in it.

4. Individuals will not engage in sharing unless they find it motivating to do so.

5. Knowledge that is transferred from other parts of the organization should be thought of as a source of inspiration—part of the knowledge-creation process—rather than as a blueprint.

6. Peer assist programs enable teams that are working on a project and need help to call on other teams or individuals with experience in the same type of task.

7. "After-action" or "lessons-learned" reviews allow a team to review what has been learned in a project immediately after completion. Questions include: What was supposed to happen? What happened? What accounts for the difference? Complete honesty is an important factor in such reviews. The information generated is applied to the next project.

8. Accessing and creating new knowledge from outside the organization is vitally important.

9. Leaders need to make knowledge building a core value and create specific opportunities and procedures by which to engage in the process (for example, using the fishbowl technique and videotaping meetings so they can be reviewed by others).

10. Leaders also must model the desired values, norms, and behaviors. They must lead the process of discussion, debate, questioning, listening, and providing feedback and closure.

What are the means by which your organization makes internal knowledge explicit and available to a wider range of people? What other means do you think it could use effectively?

EXAMPLES FROM EDUCATION

In the case of a whole school system, District 2 in New York City (see Chapter Four), we might as well be talking about Shell or Ford as we listen to Elmore and Burney (1999) describe two of the knowledge-sharing strategies employed by the district: (1) intervisitation and peer networks and (2) instructional consulting services.

Intervisitation and Peer Networks

District 2 [has] a heavy reliance on peer networks and visits to other sites, inside and outside the district, designed to bring teachers and principals into contact with exemplary practices. Intervisitation . . . and peer consultations are routine parts of the district's daily life. Teachers often visit other classrooms in conjunction with consultants' visits, either to observe one of their peers teaching a lesson or a consultant teaching a demonstration lesson. And groups of teachers often visit another school, inside or outside the district, in preparation for the development of a new set of instructional practices. Usually principals initiate these outside visits and travel with teachers.

In addition, principals engage in intervisitations with peers in other schools. New principals are paired with "buddies" who are usually more senior administrators, and they often spend a day or two each month in their first two years in their buddy's school. Groups of teachers and principals working in district initiatives travel to other districts inside and outside the city to observe specific instructional practices. And monthly districtwide principals' meetings are held on site in schools, and often principals observe individual teachers in their peers' schools as part of a structured agenda for discussing some aspect of instructional improvement. Principals are encouraged to use visits and peer advising as management strategies for teachers within their buildings. A principal who is having trouble getting a particular teacher engaged in improvement might be advised by the district staff to pair that teacher with another teacher in the building or another building in the district. And principals themselves might be encouraged to consult with other principals on specific areas where they are having difficulties.

Intervisitations and peer advising as professional development activities tend to blend into the day-to-day management of the district.

The district budgets resources to support about three hundred days of professional time to be allocated to intervisitation activities. Many such activities are not captured by these budgeted resources, since they occur informally among individuals on an ad hoc basis.

A specific example serves to illustrate how professional development and management blend together around peer advising and intervisitation. An elementary principal who is in the last year of her probationary period and is considered to be an exemplar by district personnel described off-handedly that throughout her probationary period, she had visited regularly with two other principals in the district. She is currently involved in a principals' support group that meets regularly with three other principals, and she provides support to her former assistant principal, who was recruited to take over another school as an interim acting principal. In addition this principal has led several groups of teachers from her school to observe teaching of reading and writing in university settings and in other schools in the city. She has attended summer staff development institutes in literacy and math with teachers from her school, and in the ensuing school year, she taught a series of demonstration lessons in the classrooms of teachers in her school to work out the complexities of implementing new instructional strategies. She speaks of these activities as part of her routine administrative responsibility as a principal rather than as specific professional development activities.

Another example of how peer advising and intervisitation models come together in the routine business of the district is the monthly principals' conferences. Most districts have regularly scheduled meetings of principals. . . . These routine meetings usually deal primarily with administrative business and rarely with specific instructional issues. In District 2, in contrast, regular principals' meetings—frequently called principals' conferences—are primarily organized around instructional issues and only incidentally around routine administrative business, and they often take place in the schools. At one recent principals' conference which took place in a school, the meeting principals were asked to visit classrooms, observe demonstration lessons, and use a protocol to observe and analyze classroom practice. Another recent principals' conference convened at New York's Museum of Modern Art. The theme was the development and implementation of standards for evaluating students' academic work. The conference consisted of a brief discussion of District 2's activities around standards; an overview of standards work; a series of small group discussions of an article about standards; an analysis by small groups of participants of a collection of vignettes of student work around standards; and an observation of the museum's education programs. Discussion of routine administrative business occupied less than thirty minutes at the end of the seven-hour meeting [p. 278].

In business organizations, the purposes of intergroup or departmental visitations may include (1) learning what another work group or department does and how it goes about accomplishing its work; (2) learning about the effect of one group's work on another work group or department; (3) hearing about the problems the other group faces and how it solves them; (4) learning about another group's best practices; and (5) building collegial relationships across groups and departments. Peer networks also can make a major contribution to knowledge creation and sharing in organizations.

Review the section above and try to translate the processes and examples to your own organizational setting. Similarly, see what you can learn and apply to your organization from the examples that follow. Make additional notes at the end of this chapter.

Elmore and Burney (1999) continue:

Instructional Consulting Services

District 2 invests heavily in professional development consultants who work directly with teachers individually and in groups at the school site. Over time the district has developed two main types of consulting arrangements. The first type relies on outside consultants, experts in a given instructional area who are employed under contractual arrangements. . . . The second type relies on district consultants, typically recruited from the ranks of district personnel, paid directly on the district budget, and given an assignment to work in a given instructional area. Principals and school heads play a key role in assessing the needs of the school and brokering consulting services. . . .

Overall the District 2 professional development consulting model stresses direct work by external consultants and district staff developers with individual teachers on concrete problems related to instruction in a given content area; work with grade-level teams of teachers on common problems across their classrooms; consult with individual teachers who are developing new approaches to teaching in their classrooms that other teachers might use; and work with larger groups of teachers to familiarize them with the basic ideas behind instructional improvement in a given content area. Change in instructional practice involves working through problems of practice with peers and experts, observation of practice, and steady accumulation over time of new practices anchored in one's own classroom setting.

The consulting model is labor intensive in that it relies on extensive involvement by a consultant with individuals and small groups of teachers, repeatedly over time, around a limited set of instructional problems. Connecting professional development with teaching practice in this direct way required making a choice at the district level to invest resources intensively rather than using them to provide low-impact activities spread across a larger number of teachers. The approach also implies a long-term commitment to instructional improvement in a given content area. In order to reach large numbers of teachers with the District 2 consulting model, district- and school-level priorities for professional development have to stay focused on a particular content area—in this case literacy and math—over several years so that consultants have the time to engage teachers repeatedly across a number of schools in a year and then expand their efforts to other schools in successive years [pp. 274–276].

There must be strong norms of trust and a developmental, risk-taking set of values for these methods to work. When done well and with integrity, the knowledge sharing in these kinds of settings is phenomenal.

There must be strong norms of trust and a developmental, risk-taking set of values.

Over the years, schools have built up all kinds of structural and cultural barriers to sharing, and they are having a devil of a time overcoming this inertia. Yet we are finding that teachers and principals, once they experience knowledge sharing, are thirsting for more. Let us look at a few examples from the work that Carol Rolheiser and I, at the University of Toronto, are doing with different school districts.

Assessment for Learning

The Edmonton Catholic School District has eighty-four schools. Working with an internal district steering group, Carol and I are training teams (comprising the principal and several teachers) from all eighty-four schools in four cohorts of twenty-one over a three-year period. This project is called the Assessment for Learning initiative. School teams come together with us for six to eight days annually to participate in learning about moral purpose, the change process, developing relationships and collaborative work cultures, linking parents and the community, and other topics. As the name of the initiative indicates, the teams focus particularly on what we call assessment for learning, which involves the development of school-based plans to improve student learning. School teams examine how well students are doing, what targets they should set to improve learning, and what strategies might get them where they want to go. They collect data on their own classroom practices and student performance and share these results with other school teams. At each session, the groups receive new input and share what they are doing At the end of a period of development (about a year), we hold a learning fair. The work produced, the energy in the room, and the marvel at what is going on are awesome. There is a great deal of evidence that ideas discussed in previous group sessions have been put into practice, that new ideas are being generated, and that the culture of the district is becoming more open to examining and sharing its teaching practice.

*Groups receive new input
and share what they are doing.*

The learning fair is an opportunity to showcase, reflect on, and celebrate the successes and challenges of the Assessment for Learning initiative and to share learning. Each school is invited to prepare a "storefront" that showcases its leadership work. A storefront is a visual representation of the learning that has emerged from this initiative. Participants have the opportunity to discuss their work as other schools explore the storefronts. A storefront can reflect

- Concrete actions that a leadership team has taken in the school, based on the focus of the Assessment for Learning initiative
- Artifacts that illustrate the assessment changes in the school
- Successes and outcomes of the group's work
- Challenges and solutions
- Lessons learned

Groups are encouraged to be creative in preparing their presentations (for example, they use artifacts, photographs of work in progress, graphs, charts, products, and other visuals). They also prepare brief oral descriptions to share and one-page summaries describing key activities and outcomes of their work.

The video that was produced from the event could have a tremendous multiplier effect in the schools and in other districts (provided that the principles of knowledge sharing were followed).

Early Years Literacy Project

In the Early Years Literacy Project (EYLP) in the Toronto District, which contains over six hundred schools, we are conducting nine half-days of training over a one-year period with teams of two from each of the ninety-three schools in the project. Each team consists of the principal and the literacy coordinator (a teacher leader who has a half-time appointment to work with the principal and other teachers on improving reading and writing in the school). After two half-days of training, we asked the 186 participants to fill out a one-page questionnaire that included two open-ended questions: (1) What was the strongest part of the two days? (2) What would you like to learn about in future sessions?

For both questions, the top theme in the responses pertained to knowledge sharing. For example, typical responses to the question about the strongest part of the two days were:

"Being able to dialogue with our literacy coordinator without the bump and grind of a regular school day" (from a principal)

"Discussion with other schools about how they are solving some of the issues we are facing at our school" (from a literacy coordinator)

"Focusing on what is going on in our school already (realized there is more going on than I know)" (from a literacy coordinator)

When participants were asked what they wanted in future sessions, their top request involved more dialogue and access to specific ideas:

"Need more knowledge about practice and strategies to make things happen/change in school" (from a principal)

"Would like to hear what others are doing with respect to the [project]—what does it look like, how are they interpreting data to make changes?" (from a principal)

"Reflective processes where teachers would reflect on their own personal practices and then relate to the broader picture of what others in the district were doing" (from a literacy coordinator)

Future sessions, including a learning fair of accomplishments to date, are designed to access tacit knowledge and make it available to others in the district.

All organizations would be better off (and so would society) if they strengthened their capacity to access and leverage hidden knowledge. The primary venue for this is within the work group or team and the department or functional area (or school). Sharing knowledge within these local networks is extremely important because it is when we are learning in context that knowledge becomes specific and useable. Communication in the organization within and outside these boundaries has to be encouraged, even mandated. Leaders must design and reinforce systems for the sharing of tacit and explicit knowledge, best practices, and so on. Knowledge creation and sharing must be named as a core value, and the barriers to sharing must be discovered and removed.

Barriers to sharing must be discovered and removed.

An organization that creates and shares knowledge is characterized by:

- Access to the (explicit and tacit) knowledge and skills of individuals
- People sharing the same set of beliefs about a learning culture (everyone is a teacher and a learner—at all levels)
- Professional-development opportunities in a learning community
- Communication and sharing up and down the hierarchy as well as laterally

Organizations that can achieve this will be much better at creating coherence in a disordered, nonlinear world.

Key Points from Educational Examples

1. Regularly scheduled intervisitations (to other departments or sites) and peer networks (with regularly scheduled meetings) allow people to share best practices, discuss practices and problems with colleagues and mentors, and engage in the professional development of individuals and units.

2. Organizational consulting services (with inside or outside consultants) help people deal with problems, learn how others face similar issues, and adjust to and become proficient in new practices.

3. Such techniques are based on strong norms of trust and risk-taking values.

4. Work teams can be engaged in formal learning about moral purpose, the change process, developing relationships and collaborative work cultures, and related topics. They can then share their experiences and insights with other groups.

5. It is important to make time for knowledge creation and sharing so that people do not feel that they are not accomplishing "real work."

6. Accessing and leveraging knowledge are as important as sharing it.

7. The primary venue for knowledge creation and sharing is within the work group or team and the department or functional area because it is when we are learning in context that knowledge becomes specific and useable.

8. Formal means of sharing knowledge facilitate the process. Knowledge creation and sharing must be named as a core value, and the barriers to sharing must be discovered and removed.

9. An organization that creates and shares knowledge is characterized by
   • Access to the (explicit and tacit) knowledge and skills of individuals
   • People sharing the same set of beliefs about a learning culture (everyone is a teacher and a learner—at all levels)
   • Professional-development opportunities in a learning community
   • Communication and sharing up and down the hierarchy as well as laterally
   • Lateral as well as hierarchical accountability

Note your reactions to this chapter, any insights or questions it may have generated, or any specific things you might want to refer to later.

Lessons About Creating and Sharing Knowledge

Lessons About Knowledge Is a Social Phenomenon

Write your answers to the items that follow.

1. Write your own definition of the difference between information and knowledge.

2. Think about your own work. In the space below, list a few things that you know about doing your job well (tacit knowledge) that are not part of the formal training or procedures related to your job and that you haven't shared with others.

3. Now list some things that you would like to learn about doing your job or being successful in your organization.

Lessons from Business Examples

Write your answers to the questions that follow.

4. Does your organization support people taking the time to work together and share information? If so, how?

5. Do people in your organization feel a responsibility for sharing knowledge?

6. What process exists in your organization to enable you to access the explicit and tacit knowledge of others in order to help you do your own job better?

7. How does the organizational culture affect your attempts at sharing knowledge?

8. If no particular process exists, how can you access the knowledge of others?

Lessons from Educational Examples

Write your answers to the items that follow.

9. Describe how your organization can establish or improve regularly scheduled intervisitations between work teams or departments.

10. Describe how your organization can establish or improve peer networks that allow people to share professional concerns, best practices, and other knowledge.

11. Describe how your organization can initiate or improve making mentors or counselors available to individuals in order to help them deal with issues or problems and adjust to and become proficient in new practices.

Your Personal Assessment

Write your answers to the questions that follow.

1. How have you, as an individual, typically shared tacit knowledge with others in the organizations in which you have worked?

2. If you do not typically share your tacit knowledge, why do you not do so?

3. How have you typically obtained knowledge from others in the organizations in which you have worked?

4. If you have typically not sought to obtain knowledge from others within your organization, why have you not done so?

Things to Discuss with Others

You know about peer assist programs, after-action and lessons-learned reviews, the fishbowl technique, best practices, the learning fair, and intervisitation as techniques for creating and sharing knowledge in organizations. Ask your colleagues if they know of any other such techniques, and find out how they work.

What else have you learned in this chapter that you might discuss with specific others, to your developmental benefit?

Things to Try Out

Make more detailed notes about the tacit knowledge you have about succeeding in your job, department, and organization as a whole. This information may include doing your specific job; supervising others; communicating with and relating to other persons, groups, departments, and other stakeholders within and outside the organization; and obtaining useful knowledge from a variety of sources.

Think about how such knowledge can be used in management and leadership development, succession planning, and so on, within your organization. What are the knowledge-sharing strategies that you would recommend to the organization? Create a proposal for creating and sharing knowledge throughout your organization.

What are the obstacles and enablers for this strategy? Would you need to enlist the support of someone else (a "champion") to further this endeavor?

 More Things to Try Out

Notes

Making Coherence

*In many organizations, the problem is not the absence of innovations
but the presence of too many disconnected, episodic, piecemeal projects
with superficial implementation.*

Michael Fullan

The pace of change will not slow down. Believing that the status quo is okay is unrealistic; assuming that change and complexity are constants is realistic. Change is a leader's friend, but its nonlinear messiness causes trouble. Experiencing this messiness is necessary in order to discover the hidden benefits; creative ideas and solutions are often generated when the status quo is disrupted.

Living with change means simultaneously letting go and reining in. The ultimate goal in chaotic societies is to achieve greater reining in, but the process is not as linear as most of us would like. The primary tendency of dynamic, complex systems—such as today's world—is to constantly generate overload and cause fragmentation. Leaders need to accept this condition as a given, recognize its potential value, and go about making coherence while also being aware that persistent coherence (which leads to complacency) is a dangerous thing. Fortunately, mastering the four leader capacities described in the previous chapters means not only that we can afford to let go but also that we can trust that the dynamics of change, when guided by such leadership, will be conducive to making coherence.

---

*Living with change means simultaneously
letting go and reining in.*

LEADING A LIVING SYSTEM

The basis of the new mind-set for leading in a culture of change is the realization that "the world is not chaotic; it is complex" (Pascale, Millemann, and Gioja, 2000). These authors' theory is best summarized in terms of four principles of a "living system":

1. *Equilibrium* is a precursor to *death*. When a living system is in a state of equilibrium, it is less responsive to changes occurring around it. This places it at maximum risk.
2. In the face of threat, or when galvanized by a compelling opportunity, living things move toward the *edge of chaos.* This condition evokes higher levels of mutation and experimentation, and fresh new solutions are more likely to be found.
3. When this excitation takes place, the components of living systems *self-organize* and new forms and repertoires *emerge* from the turmoil.
4. Living systems cannot be *directed* along a linear path. Unforeseen consequences are inevitable. The challenge is to *disturb* them in a manner that approximates the desired outcome [p. 6].

CREATING DISTURBANCE

The key phrase is "disturb them in a manner that approximates the desired outcome." We know that taking on all the innovations that come along or trying to reengineer people is not the kind of disturbance that is going to approximate a desired outcome.

In many organizations, the problem is not the absence of innovations but the presence of too many disconnected, episodic, piecemeal projects with superficial implementation. Schools and some organizations suffer the additional burden of having a torrent of unwanted, uncoordinated policies and innovations raining down on them from bureaucracies. Many leaders (of the pacesetter style) compound the problem with relentless "projectitis." Multiple innovations imposed simultaneously create overload, fragmentation, incoherence, and confusion, which generally are worse than the original conditions.

Thomas Hatch (2000) describes what happens "when multiple innovations collide": "It is not uncommon now to find school districts in which vastly different approaches to educational reform are being attempted at the same time. . . . In fact, in a study of 57 different districts from 1992–1995, Hess (1999) reports that the typical urban district pursued more than eleven 'significant initiatives' in basic areas such as rescheduling, curriculum, assessment, professional development and school management. . . . As a result, rather than contributing to substantial improvements, adopting improvement programs may also add to the endless cycle of initiatives that seem to sap the strength and spirit of schools and their communities" (pp. 1–2, 4). In a survey of schools in California and Texas, Hatch (2000) reports that one external provider said, "We work in schools that have seven, eight, nine affiliations with outside organizations all purporting to have something to do with reform" (p. 25).

This is not productive disturbance. Productive disturbance is likely to happen when it is guided by moral purpose and when the process creates and channels new tensions while working on a complex problem. Because the most interesting problems are complex and because there can be no advance blueprint for such cases, Heifetz (1994) says that we need adaptive leadership—"leadership without easy answers."

An organization cannot be improved only from the top. Top-down blueprinted strategies, reengineering, and relentless innovation often are more reckless than the disturbances we recommend. Most solutions cannot really be identified in advance. The people involved are a key element. The top can provide a vision, policy incentives, mechanisms for interaction, coordination, and monitoring, but to realize the vision there must be people below building capacity and shared commitment so that the moral imperative becomes a collective endeavor. Everyone has to understand and align with the big picture. The processes embedded in pursuing moral purpose, the change process, new relationships, and knowledge sharing actually produce greater and deeper coherence as they unfold. The result will be an improvement in the system.

An organization cannot be improved only from the top.

When the situation is complex, effective leaders sometimes tweak the status quo even when clear solutions are not evident. In Chapter Two, we related how Shapiro disturbed the Monsanto system through town hall meetings that unleashed a dialogue among rank-and-file members; in Chapter Four, we described how Alvarado created anxiety in School District 2 by focusing intensely on instruction and student performance data and how Welch at GE used "workout" sessions to invite employee scrutiny of existing practices. Recall the fishbowl technique used by Steve Miller of Shell (described in Chapter Five), through which people in the organization have an opportunity to observe discussion and critique proposed plans. Pascale, Millemann, and Gioja (2000) report on Miller's reflection about the processes used at Shell:

> Top-down strategies don't win too many ball games today. Experimentation, rapid learning, seizing the momentum of success works better. We needed a different definition of strategy and a different way to generate it. In the past, strategy was the exclusive domain of the CMD [Shell's chairman and his team]. But in the multi-front war Shell was engaged in, the top can't possibly have all the answers. The leaders provide the vision and are the context setters. But the actual solutions about how best to meet the challenges of the moment—those thousands of strategic challenges encountered every day—have to be made by the people closest to the action—the people at the coalface. Everyone and everything is affected.
>
> Change your approach to strategy and you change the way a company runs. The leader becomes a context setter, the designer of a learning experience—not an authority figure with solutions. Once the folks at the grassroots realize they own the problem, they also discover that

they can help create and own the answer—and they get after it very quickly, very aggressively, and very creatively, with a lot more ideas than the old-style strategic direction could ever have prescribed from headquarters. It worked because the people at the coalface usually know what's going on. They see the competitive threats and our inadequate response every day. Once you give them the context, they can do a better job of spotting opportunities and stepping up to decisions. In less than two years, we've seen astonishing progress in our retail business in some twenty-five countries. This represents around 85 percent of our retail sales volume and we have now begun to use this approach in our service organizations and lubricant business.

A program like this is a high-risk proposition, because it goes counter to the way most senior executives spend their time. When I began spending 50 to 60 percent of my time at this (with no direct guarantee that what I was doing would make something happen down the line), I raised a lot of eyebrows. People want to evaluate this against the old way which gives you the illusion of "making things happen." I encountered lots of thinly veiled skepticisms: "Did your net income change from last quarter because of this change process?" These challenges create anxiety. The temptation, of course, is to reimpose your directives and controls even though we had an abundance of proof that this would not work. The grassroots approach to strategy development and implementation doesn't happen overnight. But it does happen. People always want results yesterday. But the process and behavior that drive authentic strategic change aren't like that.

It's like becoming the helmsman of a big ship when you've grown up behind the steering wheel of a car. This approach isn't about me. It's about rigorous, well-taught marketing concepts, combined with a strong design, that enable frontline employees to think like businesspeople. Top executives and frontline employees learn to work together in partnership.

There's another kind of risk to the leaders of a strategic inquiry of this kind—and that's the risk of exposure. You're working very closely and intensely with all levels of staff, and they get to assess and evaluate you directly. Before, you were remote from them; now, you're very accessible. If that evaluation comes up negative, you've got a big-time problem.

Finally, the scariest part is letting go. You don't have the same kind of control that traditional leadership is used to. What you don't realize until you do it is that you may, in fact, have more control—but in a different fashion. You get more feedback than before, you learn more than before, you know more through your own people about what's going on in the marketplace and with customers than before. You still have to let go of the old sense of control [pp. 191–192].

"The scariest part is letting go."

Remember from Figure 1.1 that making more good things happen and preventing more bad things from happening is a process that generates widespread internal commitment from members of the organization. You can't get there from here without amplifying and working through the discomfort of disturbances. With change there will be disturbances, and this means that there will be differences of opinion that must be reconciled. Effective leadership is guiding people through the differences; in fact, it is enabling differences to surface.

If the notion of enabling disturbances bothers you, you don't have to be this radical. Working on making coherence directly is not a bad idea in a world loaded with uncertainty and confusion. But you do need to go about it by honoring the change guidelines in previous chapters, which require different views about the nature and direction of change to be identified and confronted. The only coherence that counts is not what is on paper or what top management can articulate, but what is in the minds and hearts of members of the organization.

The only coherence that counts is in the minds and hearts of members of the organization.

Key Points About Leading a Living System

1. Change and complexity are constants in today's world.

2. Living with change means simultaneously letting go and reining in.

3. Organizations are living systems. Pascale, Millemann, and Gioja (2000, p. 6) present four principles of a "living system":

   • *Equilibrium* is a precursor to *death*. When a living system is in a state of equilibrium, it is less responsive to changes occurring around it. This places it at maximum risk.

   • In the face of threat, or when galvanized by a compelling opportunity, living things move toward the *edge of chaos*. This condition evokes higher levels of mutation and experimentation, and fresh new solutions are more likely to be found.

   • When this excitation takes place, the components of living systems *self-organize,* and new forms and repertoires *emerge* from the turmoil.

   • Living systems cannot be directed along a linear path. Unforeseen consequences are inevitable. The challenge is to disturb them in a manner that approximates the desired outcome.

 Lesson About Leading a Living System

What have you learned about change in relation to living systems as a result of this book? (Include points from previous chapters as well as this one.)

MAKING COHERENCE

Leadership is difficult in a culture of change because disequilibrium is common (and valuable, provided that patterns of coherence can be forested). Complexity keeps people on the edge of chaos. It is important to be on that edge because that is where creativity resides, but anarchy lurks there too.

Making coherence includes aligning policies and coordinating strategies for changing directions, assessment, professional development, and so on.

This does not mean imposing too much order; it means not "compounding the problem by adding even greater incoherence through piecemeal reforms" (Fullan, 2003a, p. 26). Therefore, effective leaders tolerate enough ambiguity to keep the creative juices flowing, but they seek coherence along the way (once they and the group know enough). Making coherence is a perennial pursuit.

There are two concepts in complexity science that relate to making coherence: *self-organizing* and *strange attractors.* Self-organizing concerns new patterns of relationship and action that emerge when you set up the conditions and processes described in Chapters Two through Five. When you do this, the dynamics are such that the organization shifts to a new state as a result of the new interactions and ideas. Such new states represent breakthroughs in which greater coherence is achieved. This is not a leaderless proposition. Leaders in a culture of change deliberately establish innovative conditions and processes in the first place, and they guide them after that. Leaders are actually more influential in this scenario than they are with traditional, seemingly more control-based strategies. Pascale, Milleman, and Gioja (2000) advise leaders to "design more than engineer, discover more than dictate, and decipher more than presuppose" (p. 175).

Strange attractors involve experiences or forces that attract (galvanize) the energies and commitment of employees to make desirable things happen. They are strange because they are not predictable in a specific sense but, as outcomes, are likely (if not inevitable) in the processes we are describing. Visions, for example, can act as attractors, but only when they are shared at all levels of the organization and only when they emerge through experience, thereby generating commitment. Lofty visions crafted in the boardroom or on a retreat meet the "strange" criterion in the eyes of employees but not the "attractor" one.

Charismatic leaders can be strange attractors, but they generate short-term external commitment at best and dangerous dependence at worst. In his study of gurus, psychiatrist Anthony Storr (1997) warns that a charismatic leader often functions as a seductive trap to resolve the chaos we feel in complex times. What disciples get out of the relationship, he says, is the comfort of having someone else take responsibility for their decisions: "The charisma of certainty is a snare, which entraps the child who is latent in us all" (p. 233).

Effective strange attractors possess the magnetic lure of exploring moral purpose through a series of change experiences, supported by collaborative relationships that generate and sort out new knowledge.

Saying that disturbance is a good thing does not mean that coherence is not. Just the opposite is the case: unsettling processes provide the best route to greater all-around coherence. In other words, the most powerful coherence is a result of having worked through the ambiguities and complexities of hard-to-solve problems. The leader's coherence-making capacity, in this sense, is a matter of timing. There is a time to disturb and a time to cohere. Good leaders attack incoherence when it is a function of random innovation or prolonged confusion.

---

*The most powerful coherence
is a result of having worked through
the ambiguities and complexities
of hard-to-solve problems.*

There is a great deal of coherence making in Figure 1.1, from start to finish. Moral purpose sets the context: it calls for people to aspire to greater accomplishments. The standards in relation to outcomes can be very high, as they are in the cases cited in this book. These standards are also reverse drivers for achieving coherence. For example, in our work on school improvement, my colleagues and I have decided that greater assessment literacy is crucial. We define assessment literacy as consisting of the following elements:

- The capacity of teachers and principals to examine student performance data and make critical sense of them—that is, to know good work when they see it, to understand achievement scores (for example, concerning literacy), and to disaggregate data to identify subgroups that may be disadvantaged or under-performing

- The capacity to develop action plans based on the understanding gained from the data analysis in order to increase achievement

- The capacity to contribute to the political debate about the uses and misuses of achievement data in an era of high-stakes accountability

By focusing on outcomes (what students are learning), assessment literacy is a powerful coherence maker. Focusing on outcomes clarifies for teachers and principals what they are trying to accomplish and drives backward through the process toward moral purpose. It helps schools produce more coherent action plans.

This moral purpose–outcome combination won't work if we don't respect the messiness of the process required to identify best solutions and generate internal commitment from the majority of organizational members. Within the apparent disorder of the process, there are hidden coherence-making features: lateral accountability, sorting, and shared commitment:

- *Lateral accountability:* In hierarchical systems, it is easy to get away with superficial compliance or even subtle sabotage. In an interactive system, it is impossible to get away with not being noticed (poor work is noticed, and good work is more easily recognized and celebrated). There is a great deal of peer pressure along with peer support in collaborative organizations. Everyone knows that the job of making coherence is never ending and is everyone's responsibility. If people are not contributing to solutions, their inaction is more likely to stand out. The critical appraisal in such systems, whether in relation to the performance of a peer or the quality of an idea, is powerful.

---

*In hierarchical systems, it is easy
to get away with superficial compliance
or even subtle sabotage.*

- *Sorting:* A second coherence-making feature concerns the sorting process embedded in knowledge-creation and knowledge-sharing activities. The criteria for retaining an idea are (1) Does it work? and (2) Does it feed into our overall purpose? Knowledge sharing creates a continual, coherence-making sorting device for the organization.
- *Shared commitment:* The third feature involves the shared commitment to selected ideas and paths of action. People stimulate, inspire, and motivate one another to contribute and implement best ideas, and best ideas mean greater overall coherence.

Reculturing is based on trusting relationships and disciplined inquiry and action. In short, highly interactive systems with moral purpose have great cohesive powers built in; with such powers in place, what we have left to worry about are complacency, blind spots, and groupthink, so we seek new diversity and new disturbances. And the cycle continues.

Leadership in a culture of change requires a new mind-set that serves as a guide to day-to-day organizational development and performance. Leaders learn such leadership by being in organizations like the ones described in this book. Developing new leaders for a culture of change involves slow learning over time. Rapid change and slow learning: this brings us to the lesson of the hare and the tortoise in the next chapter.

Note your reactions to this chapter or any questions it may have generated here.

Key Points About Creating Disturbance

1. Taking on multiple, disconnected innovations or trying to reengineer people is not the kind of disturbance that will approximate a desired outcome.

2. Too many piecemeal projects with superficial implementation create overload, fragmentation, incoherence, and confusion.

3. Productive disturbance is likely to happen when it is guided by moral purpose and when the process creates and channels new tensions during work on a complex problem.

4. Adaptive leadership is leadership without easy answers. When the situation is complex, effective leaders sometimes tweak the status quo even when clear solutions are not evident.

5. An organization cannot be improved only from the top. The top can set the context and provide a vision, policy incentives, mechanisms for interaction, coordination, and monitoring.

6. To realize the vision, there must be people-building capacity and shared commitment, so the moral imperative becomes a collective endeavor, with everyone understanding and aligning with the big picture.

7. The processes embedded in pursuing moral purpose, the change process, relationships, and knowledge sharing produce greater coherence. The only coherence that counts is what is in the minds and hearts of members of the organization.

8. The actual solutions about how best to meet challenges have to be made by the people closest to the action—those who know what is going on. When people realize they own the problem, they discover they can help create and own the answer.

9. Change creates differences of opinion that must be identified, confronted, and reconciled. Effective leadership enables differences to surface and guides people through them.

Lessons About Creating Disturbance

Write your answers to the questions that follow.

1. Has your department or organization engaged in multiple, disconnected innovations? Has it engaged in change initiatives with superficial implementation? If so, what were the effects?

2. What do you think it means for a leader to:

   • Set a context?

   • Provide a vision?

• Provide policy incentives?

• Provide mechanisms for iteration?

3. Is any part of your department or organization in a state of equilibrium or complacency? If so, what might be done to disturb the system toward a desired outcome? What would this entail?

4. Employees, rather than managers, often are closest to the action (and the customer). What ways can you think of to tap their knowledge and involve them in the organization's search for solutions?

Key Points About Making Coherence

1. Effective leaders tolerate enough ambiguity to keep the creative juices flowing, but once they and the group know enough, they seek coherence.

2. Making coherence includes aligning policies and coordinating strategies for changing directions, assessment, and professional development.

3. Two concepts in complexity science relate to making coherence:

   - *Self-organizing* involves new patterns of relationship and action that emerge when the organization shifts to a new state as a result of the new interactions and ideas.

   - *Strange attractors* are things that attract the energies and commitment of employees to make desirable things happen. Visions can act as attractors when they are shared at all levels of the organization and when they emerge through experience, thereby generating commitment.

4. Charismatic leaders can be strange attractors, but they generate short-term external commitment at best and dangerous dependence at worst.

5. Effective strange attractors possess the lure of exploring moral purpose through a series of change experiences, supported by collaborative relationships that generate and sort new knowledge.

6. The most powerful coherence is a result of having worked through the ambiguities and complexities of hard-to-solve problems.

7. There is a time to disturb and a time to cohere. Good leaders attack incoherence when it is a function of random innovation or prolonged confusion.

8. Within the apparent disorder of the process, there are hidden coherence-making features:

   - *Lateral accountability* exists in a collaborative, interactive system in which there is peer pressure along with peer support. Everyone knows that the job of making coherence is never ending and is everyone's responsibility.

   - *Sorting* is a process embedded in knowledge creation and knowledge-sharing activities. The criteria for retaining an idea are (1) Does it work? and (2) Does it feed into our overall purpose?

   - *Shared commitment* to selected ideas and paths of action occurs when people stimulate, inspire, and motivate one another to contribute and implement best ideas. Best ideas mean greater overall coherence.

9. By focusing on outcomes, assessment literacy is a powerful coherence maker. Focusing on outcomes clarifies what people are trying to accomplish and drives backward through the process toward moral purpose. It helps produce more coherent action.

 ## Lessons About Making Coherence

Write your answers to the questions that follow.

1. In your organization:

   • Are policies aligned? Are strategies for changing direction aligned?

   • Are assessment standards defined and aligned?

   • Are opportunities for professional development consistent?

• Are the goals of policies, strategies, assessment, and professional development aligned with the organization's moral purpose (stated values) and objectives?

2. If you answered no to one or more of the above questions, make some notes at the end of this chapter about what might be done to better align these elements in order to create coherence in organizational functioning.

3. What strange attractors exist to focus the energies and commitment of employees in your organization?

4. What might serve this purpose better (for example, what series of change experiences and what conditions)?

5. Is there lateral accountability in your department or organization? If not, what can be done to develop it?

6. What is the typical sorting process for ideas in your department or organization? Is it effective? If not, how can it be improved?

7. Is there shared commitment to selected ideas and paths of action in your department or organization? If so, how was it generated? If not, what is the problem, and how might it be corrected?

Lesson About Assessment Literacy

This chapter discusses assessment literacy in school systems. But all organizations depend on data to determine organizational health, productivity, and so on. Knowing how to assess data is an important leadership skill. Rewrite the bulleted items that follow so that they describe assessment literacy in your organization. For example, you may change the wording in the following paragraph and insert your own words:

The capacity of _____ to examine _____ performance/_____ data and make critical sense of them (to know _____ when they see it, to understand _____ scores, and to disaggregate data to identify _____).

Here is how you might fill it in:

The capacity of <u>teachers and principals</u> to examine <u>student</u> performance/_____ data and make critical sense of them (to know <u>good work</u> when they see it, to understand <u>achievement</u> scores [for example, concerning literacy], and to disaggregate data to identify <u>subgroups that may be disadvantaged or underperforming</u>).

Following are some additional possibilities.

• The capacity to develop action plans based on the understanding gained from the data analysis in order to increase achievement

• The capacity to contribute to the political debate about the uses and misuses of achievement data in an era of high-stakes accountability

Your Personal Assessment

Write your answers to the questions that follow.

1. What do you feel when you think about "living on the edge of chaos"?

2. How might this affect your approach to disturbing the system?

3. How might this affect your desire to create coherence?

4. Have you initiated multiple, disconnected innovations in your department or organization? If so, what might you do now to rectify the situation?

5. Do you think that you are an adaptive leader who can create the conditions needed to "disturb the system in a manner that approximates the desired outcome" and then create appropriate coherence? What leadership characteristics might you work on in order to develop your capacity in this role?

Things to Discuss with Others

What have you learned in this chapter that you might discuss with specific others, to your developmental benefit?

Things to Try Out

Notes

Learning the Leadership

*The main mark of effective leaders
is how many effective leaders they leave behind.*

Michael Fullan

In La Fontaine's fable, the hare is quick, clever, high on hubris, and a loser. The tortoise is slow and purposeful; it adapts to the terrain and is a winner. I admit that the tortoise's way is not perfectly analogous to leading in a culture of change, because if the tortoise had known about complexity science, it might have engaged in a creative diversion or two. Still, the tortoise won, and people, like tortoises, have to stick their necks out to get somewhere.

The lessons for developing leaders in a culture of change are more tortoise-like than hare-like because they involve slow learning in context over time. This chapter presents three powerful lessons about leadership that have implications for developing more of it. Fortunately, they are interrelated: the vital and paradoxical need for slow knowing, the importance of learning in context, and the need to have leaders at all levels of the organization in order to achieve widespread internal commitment.

185

SLOW KNOWING

When talking about leading on the edge of chaos, what Claxton (1997) calls "slow knowing" becomes more important rather than less. Claxton says: "Recent scientific evidence shows convincingly that the more patient, less deliberate modes are particularly suited to making sense of situations that are intricate, shadowy or ill defined" (p. 3).

"Hare-brained" action is chasing relentless innovation.

In other words, under conditions of complex, nonlinear change, we need more slow knowing. "Hare-brained" action is chasing relentless innovation; "tortoise" action is absorbing disturbances and drawing out new patterns. Consistent with the contents of Chapter Six, Claxton (1997) observes:

> Those who try to manage nations and corporations—ministers and executives of all persuasions—may be panicked by the escalating complexity of the situations they are attempting to control into assuming that time is the one thing they have not got. Their fallacy is to suppose that the faster things are changing, the faster and more earnestly one has to think. Under this kind of pressure [they] may be driven to adopt one shallow nostrum, one fashionable idea after another, each turning out to have promised more than it was capable of delivering. Businesses are re-engineered, hierarchies are flattened, organisations try to turn themselves into learning organisations, companies become "virtual." Meetings proliferate; the working day expands; time gets shorter. So much time is spent processing information, solving problems and meeting deadlines that there is none left in which to think. Even "intuitive thinking" itself can easily become yet another fad that fails—because the underlying mindset hasn't changed [p. 214].

In referring to "hard cases" (situations of complexity), Claxton (1997) says, "One needs to be able to soak up experience of complex domains—such as human relationships—through one's pores, and to extract subtle, contingent patterns that are latent within it. And to do that one needs to be able to attend to a whole range of situations patiently without comprehension; to resist the temptation to foreclose on what that experience may have to teach" (p. 192).

Claxton talks about the poet John Keats's reference to "negative capability," which is the capability to "cultivate the ability to wait—to remain attentive in the face of incomprehension" (p. 174). Remaining attentive in the face of incomprehension respects the complexities of situations that do not have easy answers. Claxton continues, "To wait in this kind of way requires a kind of inner security; the confidence that one may lose clarity and control without losing one's self. Keats's description of negative capability came in a letter to one of his brothers, following an evening spent in discussion with his friend Charles Dilke—a man who, as Keats put it, could not 'feel he had a personal identity unless he had made up his mind about everything'" (p. 174).

Beware of leaders who are always sure of themselves. Effective leaders listen attentively; you can almost hear them listening. Ineffective leaders make up their minds prematurely and listen less thereafter. I recall someone saying about his boss, "His problem is that he is so bright, he stops listening as soon as he has understood the point." It's not a very good way to build relationships or to pick up ideas that you might have missed.

Beware of leaders who are always sure of themselves.

Paradoxically, slow knowing doesn't have to take a long time. It is more of a disposition that can be "acquired and practiced" (Claxton, 1997, p. 214). Effective leaders seem to understand this. They see the bigger picture; they don't panic when things go wrong in the early stages of a major change initiative. It is not so much that they take their time; rather, they know it takes time for things to gel. If they are attentive to the five leadership capacities, they know that things are happening all the time, even when there is no closure. In a sense, they take as much time as the situation will allow and do not rush to conclusions in order to appear decisive.

Slow knowing doesn't have to take a long time.

Instead of attacking a problem with a quick fix, what we need to do is initiate a gradual process of tweaking something, examining the results, and either giving it up or tweaking it a little more. In this way, we are not throwing the system into further chaos; things have a chance to simmer and the way to deal with them becomes more apparent. Badaracco (2002) says that "a long series of small efforts, despite its slow pace, often turns out to be the quickest way to make an organization—and the world—a better place" (p. 2).

To get good at all this takes time. Conger and Benjamin (1999) suggest a ten-year average "as the threshold time for individuals . . . to attain the status of expert" (p. 262). Of course, we all know the difference between ten years of experience and one year of experience ten times over. Therefore, the experience must be intensive and must continually cultivate the capacity to hone one's moral purpose and knowledge of nonlinear change processes, to build relationships with diverse groups, to create and share knowledge, and to strive for coherence. Most organizations do not function in a manner that provides these kinds of learning experiences. Instead, they teach people to get better at a bad game (Block, 1987). As tempting as it is, it is not sufficient to package this knowledge and try to teach it. For many reasons, it must be learned in context.

Key Points About Slow Knowing

1. The more patient, less deliberate modes of leadership are particularly suited to making sense of situations that are intricate, shadowy, or ill defined (Claxton, 1997).

2. Slow knowing involves absorbing disturbances and drawing out new patterns.

3. Slow knowing does not have to take a long time. The experience must be intensive and must continually cultivate the capacity to hone one's moral purpose and knowledge of nonlinear change processes, build relationships with diverse groups, create and share knowledge, and strive for coherence.

4. Claxton (1997) says it is a fallacy to suppose that the faster things are changing, the faster and more earnestly one has to think: "One needs to be able to soak up experience of complex domains—such as human relationships—through one's pores, and to extract subtle, contingent patterns that are latent within it. And to do that one needs to be able to attend to a whole range of situations patiently without comprehension; to resist the temptation to foreclose on what that ex-

perience may have to teach" (p. 192).

5. Negative capability is the ability to wait—to remain attentive in the face of incomprehension. Remaining attentive means listening and observing without rushing to draw conclusions, make judgments, or take action.

6. Listening attentively is key to building relationships and creating knowledge.

7. Effective leaders see the bigger picture. They don't panic when things go wrong in the early stages of a major change initiative. They know it takes time for things to gel.

8. Instead of attacking a problem with a quick fix, we need to initiate a gradual process of tweaking something, examining the results, and either giving it up or tweaking a little more.

 Lesson About Slow Knowing

What does "slow knowing" mean? Describe it in your own words.

Write a definition of "negative capability." This may be in your own words. The purpose is simply to reinforce the concept, and you will learn more if you write out your own definition before referring to the text.

LEARNING IN CONTEXT

A second lesson is that learning in context over time is essential. Aspects of this lesson are counterintuitive. Attempting to recruit and reward good people is helpful to organizational performance, but it is not sufficient. Providing a good deal of training is useful but also is a limited strategy. Elmore (2000) tells us why focusing only on talented individuals will not work:

> What's missing in this view [focusing on talented individuals] is any recognition that improvement is more of a function of *learning to do the right thing* in the setting where you work than it is of what you know when you start to do the work. Improvement at scale is largely a *property of organizations,* not of the pre-existing traits of the individuals who work in them. Organizations that improve do so because they create and nurture agreement on what is worth achieving, and they set in motion the internal processes by which people progressively learn how to do what they need to do in order to achieve what is worthwhile. Importantly, such organizations select, reward and retain people based on their willingness to engage the purposes of the organization and to ac-

quire the learning that is required to achieve those purposes. Improvement occurs through organized social learning. . . .

Experimentation and discovery can be harnessed to social learning by connecting people with new ideas to each other in an environment in which ideas are subject to scrutiny, measured against the collective purposes of the organization, and tested by the history of what has already been learned and is known [p. 25].

Learning in context over time is essential.

This is a fantastic insight: learning in the setting in which you work (in context) is learning with the greatest payoff because it is more specific (customized to the situation) and social (involves the group). Learning in context develops leadership and improves the organization as you go along; it changes the individual and the context simultaneously.

Learning in the setting in which you work
is learning with the greatest payoff.

EXAMPLES FROM EDUCATION

We return to the example of District 2 in New York City to see what learning in context means. The leadership in this district considers the development of school principals as the key to school success (think of the principal as a branch manager). The most important factor in ensuring that all students meet performance goals is the leadership of the principal. Selecting principals who are instructionally focused is a necessary first step, followed by creating an intense, comprehensive system of professional development to promote their continued growth. Comprehensive training for principals includes on-site coaching of the strategies and behaviors that principals need to use with their teachers in their classrooms to improve the learning of their students.

Opportunities for principals to learn through study groups, action research, and the sharing of experiences in support groups help to ensure that the complicated and difficult problems of instructional leadership can be addressed. High-performing districts use a monthly principals' conference as a leadership development tool. This conference is jointly planned and evaluated and creates a forum for common learning, critique, collegial sharing, and the development of a powerful culture of mutual support. Regular cross-team visitations—opportunities for mentoring in which "buddy" principals are released full time to serve as mentors or remain in their assignments (sitting) while mentoring—offer practicing principals the opportunity to work deeply on the skills and behaviors that require continual coaching. Successful districts annually increase their investment in the training of principals in order to broaden and deepen the array of leadership strategies that their site leaders possess (Fullan, Alvarado, Bridges, and Green, 2000).

The number of organizational practices in District 2 that involve principals' learning in context is impressive. These practices include:

Intervisitation: Regularly scheduled visits of principals to schools throughout the district to view implementation of initiatives

Monthly principal support groups: Monthly conferences with district instructional leaders and other principals to discuss strategies, progress toward goals, and the like

Principal peer coaching: Full-time mentor principals and selected sitting principals coaching individual principals on a regular basis

Supervisory walk-through: On-site visits by supervisors to address individual needs of schools and to provide guidance to principals

District institutes: Institutes on topics such as literacy, mathematics, standards, and assessment

Principals' study groups: Groups investigating preselected content areas or problems of practice

Individualized coaching: One-on-one coaching for individual principals, including all newly appointed principals, led by the district superintendent or principal mentors

The rationale underlying these practices and additional examples are described in Fink and Resnick (1999). The goal is to develop leaders at all levels who focus intensely on instruction and learning. Fink and Resnick emphasize that "the principal in a District 2 school is responsible for establishing a *culture of learning* in the school, one in which questions of teaching and learning provide the social life and interpersonal relations of those working in the school" (p. 5).

These learning-to-lead practices continue to be refined in the work of the Leadership Academy in San Diego, California, established in partnership with the University of San Diego. The purpose of the academy is "to comprehensively address the recruitment and development of high-quality educational leadership at all levels of the system" (Leadership Academy at University of San Diego, 2000). The Leadership Academy's goals are specifically defined:

1. Identify practitioners who have demonstrated knowledge and skill in teaching and learning, and create a newly designed certification program of theory and practice that will truly prepare graduates for the challenges of site-based leadership. University professors and outstanding leaders from San Diego City Schools, together, will develop a rigorous curriculum that incorporates the best leadership research with a full-time internship under the guidance of an outstanding principal.

2. Design and implement a program for the development of district leadership with the eight instructional leaders of San Diego City Schools. This work will include training in the development of powerful principal work plans, the design and execution of highly effective principal conferences, and the improvement of coaching skills utilized during school visits.

3. Provide training and support in the improvement of principal professional development. This work addresses the quality of the principal mentoring initiative, study groups, focused school leadership, interschool and interdistrict visitation, principals' professional development, and content learning and summer seminars and courses for further study.

Review the section above and try to transpose the examples of learning into the context of your own organizational setting. Use these examples as inspiration; write whatever seems possible or even desirable, and feel free to add any examples that you think of. Make additional notes at the end of this chapter.

With the practices described above, if you are a principal in District 2 or in San Diego, you can't help but learn to become a better leader and to foster leadership in others. In another publication, Elmore (2000) makes explicit the reasoning underlying these practices while lamenting the absence of such conditions in most school systems (and, we could add, in most other organizations):

> Unfortunately the existing system doesn't value continuous learning as a collective good and does not make this learning the individual and social responsibility of every member of the system. Leadership must create conditions that value learning as both an individual and collective good. Leaders must create environments in which individuals expect to have their personal ideas and practices subjected to the scrutiny of their colleagues, and in which groups expect to have their shared conceptions of practice subjected to the scrutiny of individuals. Privacy of practice produces isolation; isolation is the enemy of improvement.
>
> Learning requires modeling: Leaders must lead by modeling the values and behavior that represent collective goods. Role-based theories of leadership wrongly envision leaders who are empowered to ask or require others to do things they may not be willing or able to do. But if learning, individual and collective, is the central responsibility of leaders, then they must be able to model the learning they expect of others. Leaders should be doing, and should be seen to be doing, that which they expect or require others to do. Likewise, leaders should expect to have their own practice subjected to the same scrutiny as they exercise toward others [pp. 20–21].

Throughout this book, the message has been that organizations transform when they can establish mechanisms for learning in daily organizational life. As Elmore (2000) puts it, "People make . . . fundamental transitions by having many opportunities to be exposed to ideas, to argue them to their own normative belief systems, to practice the behaviors that go with those values, to observe others practicing those behaviors, and, most importantly, to be successful at practicing in the presence of others (that is, to be seen to be successful). In the panoply of rewards and sanctions that attach to accountability systems, the most powerful incentives reside in the face-to-face relationships among people in the organization, not in external systems" (p. 31).

Organizations transform
when they can establish mechanisms
for learning in daily organizational life.

Leaders in a culture of change create these conditions for daily learning. They learn to lead by experiencing such learning at the hands of other leaders. Leaders are not born; they are nurtured.

Leaders are not born; they are nurtured.

We can now see why the knowledge-sharing practices described in Chapter Five are learning in context. Peer assist programs, after-action reviews, the fishbowl technique, best practices, lessons learned, the learning fair, and intervisitation all have the quality of learning on the spot or, at least, very soon after the spot. They involve learning here and now, so that the next time will be better. These techniques are important, but they work only when leaders understand the deep cultural values that underpin them. Learning in context is an exercise in getting at tacit knowledge. It doesn't do much good, and may be harmful, to start using the techniques as products—that is, as ends in themselves—because they mask layers of hidden knowledge that are necessary for the technique to be used effectively. Techniques themselves are examples of explicit knowledge and are only the tip of the iceberg. It is much harder, and more essential, to get at the first principles: the internalized understanding that comes with knowledge derived from reflective experience with many specific situations. It is those first principles that constitute the value of the technique, not the mere use of the technique for its own sake.

Learning in context also makes it clear why and how modeling and mentoring are crucial. Mentors who evidence moral purpose, display emotional intelligence, and foster caring relationships and norms of reciprocity for knowledge sharing show the way. When leaders model and promote these values and practices in the organization, they improve the performance of the organization while simultaneously developing new leadership all the time. In this sense, organizational performance and leadership development are one and the same.

Modeling and mentoring are crucial.

If you want to develop leadership, you should focus on reciprocity—the mutual obligation and value of sharing knowledge among organizational members. The key to developing leadership is to develop knowledge and share it; if it is not mutually shared, it won't be adequately developed in the first place and will not be available to the organization in any case. For the individual, the explicit value to be internalized is the responsibility for sharing what you know. For the organization (or for leadership), the obligation is to remove barriers to sharing, create mechanisms for sharing, and reward those who do share. Leadership creates the conditions for individual and organizational development to merge.

Learning in context is based on the premise that "what is gained as a group must be shared as a group" (Pascale, Millemann, and Gioja, 2000, p. 264). Von Krogh, Ichijo, and Nonaka (2000) make a similar point:

> Allocate substantial time to think carefully through the types of knowledge you have in your business and where it resides. Is this critical knowledge for doing business kept in instructions, procedures, documents, and databases? Or is it tightly connected to the skills of individual professionals, deeply rooted in their years of experience? If the answer is yes to the second question, do these professionals operate according to care-based values, allowing younger team members to acquire their skills through mentoring processes? If yes to this question, do you recognize the role of these people in the organization, and have you given them incentives to keep contributing to the company's overall knowledge [p. 263]?

Leaders look for many opportunities to "cause" and reward leadership at all levels of the organization. When there is widespread learning in context, leadership for the future is a natural by-product.

Lesson About Learning in Context

What does "learning in context" mean? Why is learning in context important?

Key Points About Learning in Context

1. Leadership must be learned in context over time.

2. Recruiting people with particular traits and providing training are not sufficient. Organizational improvement is a function of learning to do the right thing in and for the specific work setting.

3. Improvement involves people agreeing on what they want to achieve and learning what they need to know to achieve those purposes.

4. In-context professional-development opportunities, peer discussion and support, intervisitation, mentoring, and coaching help people to learn continually and to develop as leaders.

5. Learning and sharing knowledge must become an individual and social value and the responsibility of every member of the system.

6. Environments in which personal and collective ideas and practices are scrutinized by colleagues lead to improvement.

7. Leaders must model the organization's values and the behaviors that represent them, including moral purpose, emotional intelligence, relationship building, continual learning and knowledge sharing, experimentation, and risk taking.

8. Learning in context requires getting at tacit knowledge.

9. Peer assist programs, after-action reviews, the fishbowl technique, best practices, lessons learned, the learning fair, and intervisitation all contribute to learning in context.

LEADERSHIP FOR MANY

There are two levels of the concept of leadership for many—one obvious and one more fundamental. At the obvious level, the ideas in every chapter invite all of us to practice becoming better leaders, whether we are rank-and-file employees, department heads, managers, or high-ranking executives. The more fundamental conclusion is that internal commitment cannot be activated from the top. Argyris (2000) calls internal commitment "energies internal to human beings that are activated because getting the job done is intrinsically rewarding" (p. 40). This must be nurtured up close in the daily routine of organizational behavior; for that to happen, there must be many leaders around us. Large organizations can never achieve perfect internal commitment, but with good leadership at all levels, they can generate a great deal of it, and this will feed on itself.

When Henry Mintzberg was asked what organizations have to do to ensure success over the next ten years, he replied: "They've got to build a strong core of people who really care about the place and who have ideas. Those ideas have to flow freely and easily through the organization. It's not a question of riding in with a great new chief executive on a great white horse. Because as soon as that person rides out, the whole thing collapses unless somebody can do it again. So it's a question of building strong institutions, not creating heroic leaders. Heroic leaders get in the way of strong institutions" (quoted in Bernhut, 2000, p. 23).

Leaders who are too strong or too directive do not build competence and responsibility in their followers. And building competence and responsibility may take some effort. Change involves ambiguity and anxiety, and some people may be naturally reluctant to jump into the action. As Heifetz and Linksy (2002) point out, people are torn between putting their contributions in or keeping them to themselves to avoid upsetting anyone. Leaders who demonstrate commitment to the five values described in this book, who are less sure that they are right, who are more questioning, and who are willing to search for answers to hard questions in collaboration with organizational members are best suited to leading in a culture of change. Being sure of yourself when you shouldn't be can be a liability. Decisive leaders can attract many followers, but it is usually more a case of dependence than enlightenment.

---

*The main mark of effective leaders
is how many effective leaders they leave behind.*

Strong institutions have many leaders at all levels. Those in positions to be leaders of leaders, such as the CEO, know that they do not run the place. They know that they are cultivating leadership in others; they realize that they are doing more than planning for their own succession—that if they lead right, the organization will outgrow them. The ultimate leadership contribution is to develop leaders in the organization who can move the organization even further after that leader has left (see Lewin and Regine, 2000). The main mark of effective leaders is how many effective leaders they leave behind.

A TIME TO DISTURB

As we are "careening into the future" (Homer-Dixon, 2000b, p. 6), we need leadership the most. Yet leadership in all institutions is in short supply, and worsening. "Policy Focus Converges on Leadership" (2000) begins, "After years of work on structural changes—standards and testing and ways of holding students and schools accountable—the education policy world has turned its attention to the people charged with making the system work. Nowhere is the focus on the human element more prevalent than in the recent recognition of the importance of strong and effective leadership" (p. 1).

Leadership appropriate for the times is scarce. *Leadership* and *knowledge society* are current buzzwords, and in the corporate world, the field of leadership development has become a billion-dollar business (Conger and Benjamin, 1999). In education, leadership academies abound, and many philanthropic organizations have made school leadership a top priority.

With all the attention focused on strong leaders, visions, standards, and the like, it would be easy to get this wrong. We can't solve the problem of the need to produce better leaders for a culture of change by attempting to produce greater numbers of individual leaders with the desired traits.

Glenn and Gordon (1997) state, "Today many believe it is possible to shape the future, rather than simply prepare for a future which is a linear extrapolation of the present or a product of chance or fate. [Yet the] complexity, number, and frequency of choices seem to grow beyond the ability to know and decide. Skills development in concept formulation and communications seems to be decreasing relative to the requirements of an increasingly complicated world" (p. 29).

Homer-Dixon (2000a) further reports, "Yaneer Bar-Yam, the American complexity theorist, . . . argues that the level of complexity of modern human society has recently overtaken the complexity of any one person belonging to it. . . . So as modern human society becomes more complex than we are individually, it begins to exceed our adaptive ability. In effect, we have too short a repertoire of responses to adjust effectively to our changing circumstances" (p. 211).

When responding to changing circumstances becomes this difficult, we need leaders who can combine the five core capacities discussed in this book. In a culture of complexity, the chief role of leadership is to mobilize the collective capacity to challenge difficult circumstances. Our hope is that many individuals working in concert can become as complex as the society they live in.

New contexts and new directions require both individual and system action, independently and conjointly. Individual initiative is required because we can't wait for the system to get its act together (or the system won't move unless pushed by individuals at all levels). System action is necessary because it creates new contexts, expectations, and support for individuals to change their ways (Fullan, 2003b). Sustainability includes transforming the system in a way that the conditions and capacity for continuous improvement become built in within and across the levels of reform (Fullan, 2003a).

---

*Individual initiative is required because
we can't wait for the system to get its act together.*

Key Points About Leadership for Many and a Time to Disturb

1. For an organization to be strong, leadership must be developed at all levels of the organization.

2. Individual responsibility for leading is a function of internal commitment by people who care about the organization.

3. Leaders who are too strong or heroic do not build competence and responsibility in their followers.

4. Effective leaders cultivate leadership in others. The main mark of effective leaders is how many effective leaders they leave behind.

5. The complexity of organizations is greater than the complexity or adaptability of any individual; the leader must mobilize the collective capacity to deal with difficult circumstances.

6. New contexts require both individual and system action. Individuals press the system to change, and the system creates new contexts, expectations, and support for individuals to change their ways.

7. Sustainability includes transforming the system in a way that the conditions and capacity for continuous improvement become built in within and across levels.

8. Pervasive leadership has a greater likelihood of occurring if leaders work on mastering the five core capacities: moral purpose, understanding the change process,

building relationships, creating and sharing knowledge, and making coherence. Achieving such mastery requires slow knowing and learning in context with others at all levels of the organization.

One of the main conclusions I have drawn is that the requirements of knowledge societies bring education and business leadership closer than they have ever been before. Corporations need souls, and schools need minds (and vice versa) if the knowledge society is to survive. New mutual respect and partnerships between the corporate and education worlds are needed, especially concerning leadership development, provided that those partnerships are guided by the forces discussed in Chapters Two through Six.

The capacities described in this book contain the right dynamics and the checks and balances for simultaneously letting go and reining in. When leaders act in the ways recommended, they will disturb the future "in a manner that approximates the desired outcomes" (Pascale, Millemann, and Gioja, 2000, p. 6). Such leaders will also create leadership at all levels of the organization in a way that cannot quite be controlled but that will have built-in safeguards because of the dynamics involved.

What is needed for sustainable performance is leadership at many levels of the organization. Pervasive leadership has a greater likelihood of occurring if leaders work on mastering the five core capacities: moral purpose, understanding the change process, building relationships, creating and sharing knowledge, and making coherence. Achieving such mastery is less a matter of taking leadership training and more a case of slow knowing and learning in context with others at all levels of the organization.

Ultimately, your leadership in a culture of change will be judged as effective or ineffective not by who you are as a leader but by what leadership you produce in others. Tortoises, start your engines!

Note your reactions to this chapter or any questions it may have generated here.

Lesson About Learning in Context

What does learning in context mean? Why is it important?

Your Personal Assessment

Write your answers to the questions that follow.

1. How does the fable of the hare and the tortoise apply to you? Think of an example from your own life (the context is not important). How would you do things differently today?

2. Negative capability is the ability to wait while remaining attentive. It is in contrast to those who think they must make their minds up quickly about everything, those who think they must act quickly in each situation, and those who stop listening once they think they understand something. How do you think you measure up in terms of having negative capability?

3. What can you do to further develop this capability?

4. How well do you think you model the values and behavior that you and your organization espouse?

5. How well do you think you model the values and behavior that will serve the collective good?

6. Do you ask others to do things that you are not willing or able to do?

7. Are you willing to have your own behaviors subjected to the same scrutiny as you exercise toward others?

Things to Discuss with Others

Ask some of your colleagues whether they have ever learned more about a situation by going slowly rather than by deciding or acting immediately. Ask them what they think of the concept of slow knowing in terms of leadership development.

What else have you learned in this chapter that you might discuss with specific others, to your developmental benefit?

Things to Try Out

Pick a complex or ill-defined situation that seems appropriate and try being a tortoise instead of a hare. Rather than making your mind up right away and jumping into action, try to "remain attentive in the face of incomprehension," to allow yourself to see the subtleties of the situation and the patterns that emerge over time. Keep notes as you do this about your own feelings and behaviors, as well as about what happens over time.

 ## Other Things to Try Out

ANSWER: Lesson About Learning in Context

What does learning in context mean? Why is learning in context important?

Learning in the setting in which you work (in context) is learning with the greatest payoff because it is more specific (customized to the situation) and because it is social (involves the group). Learning in context develops leadership and improves the organization as you go along; it changes the individual and the context simultaneously.

Notes

Optional Exercise

This exercise is an opportunity for you to try out what you have learned in this book about leading in a culture of change. As you work through the steps, practice the five core capacities of effective change leaders.

1. Think of an existing problem or condition that propels change in your organization. Describe the existing problem or condition as specifically as possible in the space below.

2. List as many reasons for or indications of the problem or condition as you can.

3. Of the reasons or conditions listed, which do you think is most at the heart of the problem?

4. Are you the only one who has defined the problem or condition and identified its causes? Have you discussed it with others who are affected by it? Have you asked them to consider it and tell you what they think the causes are?

5. If you have not, do so now. Use some of the techniques you have learned to gather information and opinions from various stakeholders. Then return to the exercise.

6. Do their responses support your initial assessment? If not, modify your assessment in terms of what you have learned.

7. What might be done to "solve" the problem or adapt to the condition? Take some time to discuss this with the people who are affected by it and (if a different group) with those who will be implementing the solution or adaptation. In discussing this with others, you may wish to consider the following:

• What is the goal and nature of the "solution" or adaptation (the change)?

• How will it be introduced?

• How will it be led (by whom, at what level)?

• What will the components of the initiative be? Briefly describe what might change or be abandoned; what new processes, procedures, or practices might be initiated; and who might do each thing.

• Who might be responsible for implementing it?

Remember to continually assess your behavior and the discussion of this initiative in terms of the five basic components of change leadership. For example, how do you communicate and exemplify moral purpose? How do you use your knowledge of the change process? How do you build relationships? How do you structure and encourage the creation and sharing of knowledge? How do you disturb the system and (understanding the four principles of living systems) also make coherence?

8. Assess the proposed initiative or solution in terms of what you know about slow knowing.

9. What can you do from here on with the ideas and possibilities that have been generated during these discussions and explorations?

Writings by Well-Known Authors Support the Concepts Presented
in *Leading in a Culture of Change*

In four volumes of contemporary writings from the Peter F. Drucker
Foundation's Leader to Leader series (published by Jossey-Bass in
2002 and edited by F. Hesselbein and R. Johnston), common themes
consistently reinforce the concepts presented in *Leading in a Culture
of Change*. These volumes are *On Mission and Leadership, On Leading
Change, On High Performance Organizations*, and *On Creativity, Innovation, and Renewal*. As you read this synopsis of chapters by re-
spected leaders in the business community and in the fields of
leadership, management, organization development, and change, you
will notice the agreement between their messages and those presented
in this book. In addition, the beliefs conveyed in this synopsis will help
to reinforce what you have just learned or relearned.

The common themes in the series are as follows.

LEADER CHARACTER AND ORGANIZATIONAL VALUES

Overwhelmingly, the articles in this collection emphasize the importance of values
as organizational and personal imperatives. In other words, being "good" is good
business. A primary conclusion is that effective leaders have exemplary character

and the ability to motivate people to greater performance by imparting a sense of mission and significance to the work they do. Bennis states that a moral compass, or character, is the key to leadership. Roddick maintains that the leader and the organization must have a moral agenda. Goleman speaks of the importance of integrity, conscientiousness, and trustworthiness in a leader. Lencioni points to the need for character, authenticity, humility, and charisma to engender trust, loyalty, and inspiration. Hesselbein urges leaders to ensure that their lives are consistent with the values and mission of the organization they are building. Komisar says that leadership resides in character and that leadership is about inspiring and motivating and allowing people to realize the greatness in themselves rather than demonstrating the leader's greatness.

As a leader, Knowling does not want to "wake up one day with a profitable organization that does not have a soul." Ulrich, Smallwood, and Zenger remind us that leaders who achieve results but lack integrity, character, and values face the challenge of winning the support necessary for long-term performance. Several authors mention the dysfunctional results of leaders who are arrogant, self-promoting, competitive, and interested only in the bottom line.

Communicating Organizational Mission and Values and Helping Others to See How Their Work Makes a Difference

Bennis says that leaders must help people to see the contribution their work makes. Goleman says that the purpose of a leader is to safeguard the organization's mission and serve the common good. Roddick and Pinchot agree that people want to be engaged in and accomplish something that is deeply meaningful to them. Hock says that followership is evoked by a clear, compelling purpose and ethical principles that are shared by all. Pollard maintains that people want to contribute to a cause, to have purpose and meaning in their work; seeing purpose and opportunity in one's work unleashes creative power, productivity, quality, and value. Bartlett agrees that people need to see meaning in their work, to belong and contribute to an institution that makes a difference. Kanter talks about communicating an aspiration, an appeal to people's better selves. Lipman-Blumen says that connective leaders invite those around them to join their quest for greater meaning. According to Kotler, leaders must be able to stretch the sights of their followers to embrace a worthy goal—one that is expressed not in financial terms but in social-benefit terms—and show how people's everyday work contributes to the goal. Berry's research reveals the importance of integrity, generosity, excellence, social profit, and other values and a cause around which people can organize their efforts. Komisar says that the way to make business work in the long term is to humanize it. Senge notes that if people enjoy their work, they will innovate, take risks, and trust one another because they are committed to what they are doing.

Creating a Climate of Openness, Optimism, and Trust

Openness relates to communication going in all directions in the organization, from the bottom up and across divisions, as well as from the top down. Optimism and hope generate energy and sustain motivation. Trust is based on a number of factors, including candid communication and enough stability in the midst of change to allow people to get on with their work.

Weick, Sutcliffe, and Obstfeld state that a climate of openness makes people more willing to report and discuss errors and to work at correcting them. Hamel and Skarzynski point out that people must feel safe before they will express divergent or innovative ideas. Bennis emphasizes the need to create and sustain trust through congruity and a climate of candor that allows problems to be discussed both upward and downward. He also stresses the need to create an atmosphere of hope to sustain forward momentum and commitment. Roddick notes the importance of communicating with everybody in the organization and of remaining hopeful and creative. Goleman says that one of the most important motivational abilities is optimism. Especially in times of change, according to Pollard, people need hope. Mintzberg commends the inspirational manager's "straightforward" style and "upbeat" nature. Champy says that effective achievers show persistence, preparation, clarity of purpose, and optimism.

Mintzberg describes inspirational managers who create the conditions that foster openness and release energy. He makes the point that when people are trusted, they do not have to be empowered. Brown says that to nurture creativity, we must listen and elicit the cross-currents of doubt, debate, and exploration that surround any new idea. Leaders in Knowling's organization build trust by talking honestly.

Drucker views preserving trust as especially important in times of change and believes that the way to do this is to preserve the organization's values. Steere and Kotler agree that meaningful growth and change cannot be sustained in the absence of trust.

Encouraging Meaningful Personal Development

Roddick notes that when leaders develop a process of education in a company, especially one that taps into people's values, those people don't want to leave. Goleman lists coaching and development of others as key leadership skills. Tichy reminds us that people need ongoing opportunities to use their skills, try new things, and stretch their limits.

Brown says that leaders must find ways to foster intellectual capital that becomes inextricably bound to a sense of personal meaning. According to Pollard, the workplace must become a place of training and education, and the organization's mission must be in alignment with people's growth and development. He says that a leader's task is to train and motivate people so they will "be more productive in their work and, yes, even be better people." The leader's job, notes Bartlett, has to shift from administrative controller to developmental coach, to provide those on the front line with the resources, capability, and self-discipline to manage their new autonomy. Self-discipline, he adds, is far different from, and much more powerful than, compliance.

Many of the authors in this series describe the need to develop and reward entrepreneurial talent within an organization. Kanter says that change leaders transfer ownership of change projects to teams of workers and then support, coach, and reward them. Sull quotes McKinsey's principle of "developing and exciting people" through "active apprenticeship and stretching, entrepreneurial opportunities." Hesselbein cites job expansion, job rotation, and innovative opportunities for development as ways to release the energies of people and increase job satisfaction.

Lipman-Blumen says that connective leaders amplify their supporters' abilities and entrust them with challenging tasks, thereby spurring their personal growth. They train a large cadre of potential successors to ensure that talented people succeed them. They set high expectations, entrust valued tasks to others, and avoid micromanaging so that others' creativity can expand to its natural limit. O'Toole, Pasternack, and Bennett describe effective leaders who set goals, create the context in which capable individuals can find their own best paths, and leave it up to them to creatively come up with ways to achieve those goals.

Building a Sense of Community Within the Organization

The term *community* may relate to the organizational community or to the larger social environment in which it operates. Leader to Leader authors agree that a positive identification with both is necessary for a healthy organization.

Goleman says that the strongest predictors of performance are the harmony of the group, the trust of the group, and the sense of team identification. Pollard raises the issue of organizations being moral communities that help shape the character and behavior of their people. With missions that provide organizing principles, he says, organizations become communities of people caring for one another and for those they serve. Hock adds that true leaders symbolize, legitimize, and strengthen behavior in accordance with the sense of the community and enable its shared purpose, values, and beliefs to emerge. Mintzberg warns that antisocial, mercenary models of management will doom organizations. Bartlett reminds us that organizations are not just economic entities; they are also social institutions, and for many people, much of the meaning in life comes from their engagement in their workplace. Pinchot states that commitment, innovation, and energy grow only in a healthy community of work in which status is gained by giving away something (for example, knowledge, expertise) and people are willing to cooperate across boundaries because they share common purposes. Brown says that leaders must focus on the shared sense of place that increasingly defines the quality of work life. Nicholson describes a crisis in leadership selection and says that the solution is nothing less than a culture change that restores some sense of community.

Lipman-Blumen says that to build community in organizations, connective leaders take the broadest perspective on what is needed and by whom. They search for common ground and encourage collaboration. She notes that building community requires an appreciation of obscured long-term possibilities and that it takes vision and courage to choose between current demands and a better future for a larger community.

Making a Contribution to the Larger Community

Roddick describes a new measure of organizational success based on social values and cites the need to see business as a community of peoples. Tichy says that leaders must expand their view of the organization's role in society; he cites Nasser's view of the business benefits of an engaged workforce. Kotler stresses the leaders' need to market social ideas. Adams refers to "enlightened capitalism."

QUESTIONING, EXPERIMENTING, AND LEARNING FROM MISTAKES

One volume of the series focuses on change and another addresses innovation and renewal; however, there are many areas of crossover. Although change may be a response to considerations or events external to an organization, much change, innovation, and renewal are generated within the organization, even if the impetus to initiate them is an awareness of external change.

Pascal and Nicholson remind us that natural selection operates by favoring traits that assist survival and reproduction and eliminating those that do not. Several authors note the human tendencies that can get in the way of this process in social systems.

One of the primary skills leaders can encourage is appropriate questioning regarding the status quo. Mintzberg, citing Ralph Stacey, states that cultures of dependence and conformity obstruct the questioning and complex learning that encourage innovative action. Sull cites McKinsey's principle of upholding "the obligation to dissent."

Organizations must regularly examine what they have done, how it has been done, and for whom, and then decide what needs to be dropped, done differently, or replaced. Weick, Sutcliffe, and Obstfeld and other authors call for the questioning of assumptions and procedures to fight complacency and rigidity. Tichy notes that past practices and assumptions can forestall growth. Hesselbein, Kanter, Sull, Steere, and Markides urge leaders to examine and challenge the way in which things have been done—prevailing assumptions, conventional wisdom, policies, practices, procedures, and products—even when they are profitable and to keep only those that reflect the desired future. Senge adds that this is the difference between creating proactively and problem solving reactively. Several authors mention the role that serendipitous encounters with peers, customers, and others can play.

Bartlett says that leaders need to create dynamic disequilibrium, challenge the organization's working assumptions, and create the discomfort that prompts creative action. Nasser agrees that some instability is needed to produce creative and innovative approaches to growing the organization. Gould says that a degree of randomness helps systems to find their best adaptive form. Pascale says that equilibrium makes a system less responsive to change and threat and that living things move toward the edge of chaos, creating upheaval but not dissolution, in order to effect productive change when galvanized by a compelling opportunity. Then they experiment, self-organize, and revitalize themselves to take advantage of opportunities. The challenge is to disturb them toward the desire outcome and then correct course as the outcome unfolds.

Bennis, Goleman, and Maletz and Katzenbach note the importance of the leader in learning from successes and accepting setbacks, learning from them, carrying on, and inspiring others to do the same. Lipman-Blumen describes leaders who support others despite occasional failures and encourage them to try again. Weick, Sutcliffe, and Obstfeld note the need to give individuals the opportunity to build expertise, notice and correct errors, and apply their learnings to new problems. O'Toole, Pasternack, and Bennett talk about giving people the resources to succeed and the freedom to fail without penalty. Leonard and Swap say that only leaders who encourage others to distinguish between intelligent failures and stupid mistakes—and who reward the former—are likely to encourage creativity. They call this "falling forward." Brown says that we learn far more from failures than from successes.

Hesselbein and several other authors also mention the need to focus on the few initiatives that will make a difference rather than spreading the organization too thin.

Seeking Diversity of Experience and Opinion

Senge refers to the need to develop diversity of thought as well as demographic diversity. Berry says that the workforces of top-performing companies are demographically, educationally, ethnically, and socially diverse. Nasser holds that diversity results in a more creative and vital culture. Weick, Sutcliffe, and Obstfeld believe that a group with diverse perceptions has more information at its disposal. Leonard and Swap maintain that only diversity of working and thinking styles, professional and personal experience, education, and culture can create the range of options required for true creativity.

Lawrence notes that employee participation is essential to quality improvement and organizational performance, and he exhorts organizations to form partnerships with all stakeholders, not only to improve delivery of services but also to learn from them. He tells how Kaiser reconfigured its board to bring in a broader range of perspectives and expertise, in the belief that the ability to collect, manage, and make sense of available information is key. To help create perspective, Bartlett and others stress the need to seek and encourage feedback and innovation from the bottom up, to listen to the people on the front line, who know what is really going on. Knowling agrees that leaders must connect with customers, suppliers, and other partners, as well as front-line employees, in order to learn from them important things that they would never know otherwise.

Grove warns that unless leaders welcome the input of people in the lower ranks of the organization and contrarian views, they may never hear from those who can help them respond quickly to major change. Steere agrees that leaders must be able to listen to diverse points of view and remain open to conflicting or even painful information, to keep them from becoming complacent and insular and losing flexibility and awareness of the marketplace.

Pascale warns that the survival of any organism depends on its ability to cultivate (not just tolerate) variety in its internal structure. Failure to do so leads to inability to cope successfully with variety when it is introduced from the outside. Gould says that diversity provides resiliency against catastrophe.

Focusing on the Customer

Hesselbein recommends gaining input from those affected by decisions as well as from those implementing them. She and Adams note that listening to the customer has become the common focus of organizations in all sectors. Kanter recommends that leaders create channels for managers, salespeople, service representatives, and receptionists to share what customers are saying about products and services. Grove and Kotler stress the need to acknowledge the reality of the market—what both old customers and potential new customers want—and to respond to the demands of specific customer groups. Tichy calls this looking at the organization from the outside—at what customers and the environment require and at potential new ways to serve new customers. Seybold identifies those who reinvent their industries—focusing on customer convenience—as the leaders of the twenty-first century.

Slywotzky notes that successful companies focus on customers rather than on their product or technology; they regularly identify their most important customers—the ones who will have the greatest impact on future success in the industry—and build their next-generation business models around those customers. Many authors would agree with Kotler's statement that great products and services are designed in the marketplace, with customers taking the lead in expressing their needs and assisting organizations in developing solutions.

ANTICIPATING CHANGE, STAYING AGILE AND FLEXIBLE, AND FORMULATING PLANS BASED ON THE MISSION

Although there are three distinct themes here, they are interrelated. Lawrence reminds us that one way to respond to a rapidly changing marketplace is to integrate services and make pertinent information quickly available to all. Knowling and Hesselbein both stress the importance of anticipating change, being fluid, learning to deal with ambiguity, and being able to change the business model to meet changes in the market and economy, all while having an overarching vision and values to guide such change. Sull recommends an operating philosophy that guides employees while leaving sufficient flexibility to respond to shifts in customer demands and technology.

Drucker and Senge emphasize the importance of anticipating change, being open to it, and building a culture that welcomes it. Nasser refers to the need to embrace change and says that most business failures occur because leadership does not respond to long-term social and economic forces. Kotler calls this being able to tease out opportunities initially that might appear to be threats.

Kanter says that leaders must monitor external reality through a variety of means and be attentive to early signs of discontinuity, disruption, threat, and opportunity in the marketplace and the community. Steere and Weick, Sutcliffe, and Obstfeld remind us that leaders must anticipate and influence some changes and be able to react effectively (resiliently) to others. In agreement with Drucker and Senge, Steere adds that leaders must be comfortable dealing with change and that those who seek permanence and stability, or who can work only in a clearly defined hierarchy, are out of synch with today's business challenges. Maletz and Katzenbach and Duarte and Snyder describe the need for managers to become flexible and adept at operating in a changing environment. Drucker and Senge urge us to welcome surprise and to view change, even a surprise or an unexpected success, as an opportunity rather than a threat. Rubin agrees and notes that change cannot be controlled; it needs to be treated more like an uninvited guest.

Lencioni describes a successful leader's steady, persistent drive for results regardless of the challenges that arise. Hock exhorts leaders to think, judge, act, and free others to do the same. Markides says that strong leaders have the courage to abandon the status quo in order to achieve an uncertain future. Many authors note that the leader's job is to remove obstacles and constraints, to prevent problems that would get in the way of people's ability to achieve, rather than focusing on solving or "fixing" problems. Mintzberg exhorts leaders to infuse slow, profound change (not the traumatic or superficial change often seen in organizations) while holding other things steady to create consistency and reliability.

ORGANIZATIONAL SYSTEMS AND CHANGE

Several authors note the ways in which organizations are and are not like living organisms in their responses to outside disturbances and their processes of change.

Seybold informs us that people's nervous systems take three years to learn new behaviors that supplant old ones and that organizations can't change faster than people can learn. This is one reason that start-ups are able to evolve quickly, while established institutions move more slowly.

Pascale maintains that machine-age principles prompt stagnation and decline in the face of continuous change. Organizations, he says, must behave like living organisms, avoiding equilibrium, cultivating diversity, fostering entrepreneurial initiatives, consolidating learning, and reorganizing to move rapidly to exploit winning positions in the marketplace.

Bridges and Mitchell, Grove, and Pascale all agree with Kanter that the difficult part of change is the middle, where initiatives can become derailed, and encourage leaders to have patience and persevere and to recognize and reward accomplishments.

Hock says that human ingenuity is underutilized and abused as a result of mechanistic, industrial-age "dominator" concepts of organization and the management practices they spawn. He exhorts us to redefine our views of leadership and followership. Bartlett states that models of management built around strategy, structure, and systems are now failing because today's scarce resources are the information, knowledge, and expertise necessary to compete. The new management philosophy, he says, is based on purpose, process, and people. Leaders must spend more time assembling the teams to link people and resources across the organization and must create the channels of communication that support cross-unit decision making and foster learning. They must shift their focus from managing strategic content to framing organizational and behavioral contexts, creating a sense of stretch, self-discipline, trust, and support. Senge warns against applying the machine metaphor of the industrial age (steering, controlling, and repairing) to people. He also notes that mechanistic thinking leads to assembly-line homogeneity, whereas today's organizations need many eyes focused in different directions.

Bridges and Mitchell speak of person-centered leadership. Conger notes that access to information, new worker attitudes, and the increasing autonomy of people in the middle and front lines of organizations all contribute to a shift away from decision making and control residing in top-down hierarchies. Hesselbein; O'Toole, Pasternack, and Bennett; and Pinchot recommend dispersing the responsibilities of leadership across the organization at every level and creating flexible, fluid structures and systems that unleash people's energies and entrepreneurial behavior. Pinchot calls this a community of work.

Nasser talks about creating an environment that gives people autonomy to determine how best to meet the organization's business objectives. Champy says that the best way to keep control is to share it. Passion and commitment are cemented when decision-making authority and personal rewards are widely distributed. Weick, Sutcliffe, and Obstfeld report that high-reliability organizations recognize that expertise and experience are more important than rank; they allow decision making and troubleshooting to migrate to people who may have more relevant expertise.

Nicholson cites the need for leaders who are less traditional bosses than they are orchestrators, collaborators, and facilitators. Steere, O'Toole, Pasternack, and Bennett, and other authors remind us that leaders can cultivate and influence but not control the behaviors of people and markets and that trying to force compliance rarely produces outstanding results.

With your understanding of the framework for leadership presented in Figure 1.1 and the components of the five leader capacities, you no doubt recognize the themes of moral purpose, understanding change, building relationships, creating and sharing knowledge, making coherence, and energy, enthusiasm, and hope, as well as the many specific practices inherent in each of them. In this rapidly changing world, it may be comforting to know that, at least for now, there are some things that a leader can learn and do that will help his or her organization—and the people in it—not only to weather the storms of change, but even to help steer the vessel.

REFERENCES

Argyris, C. *Flawed Advice and the Management Trap.* New York: Oxford University Press, 2000.

Badaracco, J. *Leading Quietly.* Boston: Harvard Business School Press, 2002.

Barber, M. "High Expectations and Standards." Unpublished manuscript, Department for Education and Employment, London, 2000.

Beer, M., Eisenstat, R., and Spector, B. *The Critical Path to Corporate Renewal.* Boston: Harvard Business School Press, 1990.

Bernhut, S. "Henry Mintzberg in Conversation." *Ivey Business Journal,* Sept.–Oct. 2000, pp. 19–23.

Bernstein, P. *Against the Gods.* New York: Wiley, 1996.

Bishop, B. *The Strategic Enterprise.* Toronto: Stoddart, 2000.

Black, J. S., and Gregersen, H. *Leading Strategic Change.* Upper Saddle River, N.J.: Pearson Education, 2002.

Block, P. *The Empowered Manager: Positive Political Skills at Work.* San Francisco: Jossey-Bass, 1987.

Bolman, L., and Deal, T. *Escape from Cluelessness.* New York: AMACOM, 2000.

Brown, J. S., and Duguid, P. *The Social Life of Information.* Boston: Harvard Business School Press, 2000.

Bryk A., and Schneider, B. *Trust in Schools.* New York: Russell Sage Foundation, 2002.

Bryk, A., and others. *Charting Chicago School Reform.* Boulder, Colo.: Westview Press, 1998.

"Charisma and Loud Shouting." *Times Education Supplement,* Nov. 10, 2000, p. 28.

Claxton, G. *Hare Brained and Tortoise Mind.* London: Fourth Estate, 1997.

Collins, J. *Good to Great.* New York: HarperCollins, 2001.

Conger, J. A., and Benjamin, B. *Building Leaders: How Successful Companies Develop the Next Generation.* San Francisco: Jossey-Bass, 1999.

Darrah, C. "Workplace Training, Workplace Learning: A Case Study." *Human Organization,* 1993, *54*(1), 31–41.

De Gues, A. *The Living Company.* Boston: Harvard Business School Press, 1997.

Dinkmeyer, D., and Eckstein, D. *Leadership by Encouragement.* Delray Beach, Fla.: St. Lucie Press, 1996.

Dixon, N. *Common Knowledge.* Boston: Harvard Business School Press, 2000.

Earl, L., and others. *Watching and Learning: OISE/UT Evaluation of the Implementation of the National Literacy and Numeracy Strategies.* London: Department for Education and Employment, 2000.

Egan, G. *Change Agent Skills A: Assessing and Designing Excellence.* San Diego, Calif.: University Associates, 1988a.

Egan, G. *Change Agent Skills B: Managing Innovation and Change.* San Diego, Calif.: University Associates, 1988b.

Elmore, R. F. *Building a New Structure for School Leadership.* Washington, D.C.: Albert Shanker Institute, 2000.

Elmore, R. F., and Burney, D. "Investing in Teacher Learning: Staff Development and Instructional Improvement." In L. Darling-Hammond and G. Sykes (eds.), *Teaching as the Learning Profession: Handbook of Policy and Practice.* San Francisco: Jossey-Bass, 1999.

Fink, E., and Resnick, L. "Developing Principals as Instructional Leaders." Paper prepared for the High Performance Learning Communities Project, Learning Research and Development Center, University of Pittsburgh, 1999.

Fullan, M. *Change Forces: Probing the Depths of Educational Reform.* London: RoutledgeFalmer, 1993.

Fullan, M. *Change Forces: The Sequel.* New York: RoutledgeFalmer, 1999.

Fullan, M. *Leading in a Culture of Change.* San Francisco: Jossey-Bass, 2001a.

Fullan, M. *The New Meaning of Educational Change.* (3rd ed.) New York: Teachers College Press, 2001b.

Fullan, M. *Change Forces with a Vengeance.* New York: RoutledgeFalmer, 2003a.

Fullan, M. *The Moral Imperative of School Leadership.* Thousand Oaks, Calif.: Sage, 2003b.

Fullan, M., Alvarado, A., Bridges, R., and Green, N. *Review of Administrative Organization: Guilford County.* Toronto: Ontario Institute for Studies in Education, 2000.

Galbraith, J. K. "Stop the Madness." *Toronto Globe and Mail,* July 6, 2002, p. 38.

Garten, J. *The Mind of the CEO.* New York: Basic Books, 2001.

Garvin, D. *Learning in Action.* Boston: Harvard Business School Press, 2000.

Gaynor, A. "A Study of Change in Educational Organizations." In L. Cunningham (ed.), *Educational Administration.* Berkeley, Calif.: McCutcheon, 1977.

Gladwell, M. *The Tipping Point.* Boston: Little, Brown, 2000.

Gleick, J. *Faster: The Acceleration of Just About Everything.* New York: Pantheon Books, 1999.

Glenn, J., and Gordon, T. (eds.). *State of the Future: Implications for Action Today.* Washington, D.C.: American Council for the United Nations University, 1997.

Goffee, R., and Jones, G. "Why Should Anyone Be Led by You?" *Harvard Business Review,* Sept.-Oct. 2000, pp. 63–70.

Goleman, D. *Emotional Intelligence.* New York: Bantam Books, 1995.

Goleman, D. *Working with Emotional Intelligence.* New York: Bantam Books, 1998.

Goleman, D. "Leadership That Gets Results." *Harvard Business Review,* Mar.-Apr. 2000, pp. 78–90.

Goleman, D., Boyatzis, R., and McKee, A. *Primal Leadership.* Boston: Harvard Business School Press, 2002.

Hamel, G. *Leading the Revolution.* Boston: Harvard Business School Press, 2000.

Hatch, T. *What Happens When Multiple Improvement Initiatives Collide.* Menlo Park, Calif.: Carnegie Foundation for the Advancement of Teaching, 2000.

Havelock, R. G. *The Change Agent's Guide to Innovation in Education.* Englewood Cliffs, N.J.: Educational Technology Publications, 1973.

Heifetz, R. *Leadership Without Easy Answers.* Cambridge, Mass.: Harvard University Press, 1994.

Hesselbein, F., and Johnston, R. (eds.). *On Creativity, Innovation, and Renewal.* San Francisco: Jossey-Bass, 2002a.

Hesselbein, F., and Johnston, R. (eds.). *On High Performance Organizations.* San Francisco: Jossey-Bass, 2002b.

Hesselbein, F., and Johnston, R. (eds.). *On Leading Change.* San Francisco: Jossey-Bass, 2002c.

Hesselbein, F., and Johnston, R. (eds.). *On Mission and Leadership.* San Francisco: Jossey-Bass, 2002d.

Hess, F. M. *Spinning Wheels: The Politics of Urban School Reform.* Washington, D.C.: Brookings Institution, 1999.

Homer-Dixon, T. *The Ingenuity Gap.* New York: Knopf, 2000a.

Homer-Dixon, T. "Leadership Captive." *Toronto Globe and Mail,* Nov. 24, 2000b, p. A15.

Kotter, J. *Leading Change.* Boston: Harvard Business School Press, 1996.

Kotter, J., and Cohen, D. *The Heart of Change.* Boston: Harvard Business School Press, 2002.

Kouzes, J. M., and Posner, B. Z. *Encouraging the Heart: A Leader's Guide to Rewarding and Recognizing Others.* San Francisco: Jossey-Bass, 1998.

Leadership Academy at University of San Diego. *San Diego: Joint Initiative of the San Diego School District and the University of San Diego.* San Diego, Calif.: Leadership Academy at University of San Diego, 2000.

Lewin, K. "Frontiers in Group Dynamics: I. Concept, Method, and Reality in Social Sciences: Social Equilibria and Social Change." *Human Relations,* 1947, *1*(1), 5–41.

Lewin, R., and Regine, B. *The Soul at Work.* New York: Simon & Schuster, 2000.

Lortie, D. *School Teacher: A Sociological Study.* Chicago: University of Chicago Press, 1975.

Marion, R. *The Edge of Organization.* Thousand Oaks, Calif.: Sage, 1999.

Maurer, R. *Beyond the Wall of Resistance.* Austin, Tex.: Bard Books, 1996.

McLaughlin, M., and Talbert, J. *Professional Communities and the Work of High-School Teaching.* Chicago: University of Chicago Press, 2001.

Mintzberg, H., Ahlstrand, B., and Lampel, J. *Strategy Safari: A Guided Tour Through the Wilds of Strategic Management.* New York: Free Press, 1998.

Newmann, F., King, B., and Youngs, P. "Professional Development That Addresses School Capacity." Paper presented at the annual meeting of the American Educational Research Association, New Orleans, Apr. 2000.

Nonaka, I., and Takeuchi, H. *The Knowledge-Creating Company.* New York: Oxford University Press, 1995.

Palmer, P. *The Courage to Teach.* San Francisco: Jossey-Bass, 1998.

Pascale, R., Millemann, M., and Gioja, L. *Surfing the Edge of Chaos.* New York: Crown, 2000.

Peters, T., and Waterman, R. *In Search of Excellence.* New York: HarperCollins, 1982.

"Policy Focus Converges on Leadership." *Education Week,* Jan. 12, 2000, pp. 1, 17.

Polyani, M. *The Tacit Dimension.* Gloucester, Mass.: Peter Smith, 1983.

Reina, D., and Reina, M. *Trust and Betrayal in the Workplace.* San Francisco: Berrett-Koehler, 1999.

Ridley, M. *The Origins of Virtue.* Harmondsworth, England: Penguin Books, 1996.

Senge, P., and others *Schools That Learn.* New York: Doubleday, 2000.

Sergiovanni, T. J. *The Lifeworld of Leadership: Creating Culture, Community, and Personal Meaning in Our Schools.* San Francisco: Jossey-Bass, 1999.

Sober, E., and Wilson, D. *Unto Others: The Evolution and Psychology of Unselfish Behavior.* Cambridge, Mass.: Harvard University Press, 1998.

Stacey, R. *Strategic Management and Organizational Dynamics.* (3rd ed.) Upper Saddle River, N.J.: Prentice Hall, 2000.

Stein, S., and Book, H. *The EQ Edge.* Toronto: Stoddart, 2000.

Storr, A. *Feet of Clay: A Study of Gurus.* London: HarperCollins, 1997.

Von Krogh, G., Ichijo, K., and Nonaka, I. *Enabling Knowledge Creation: How to Unlock the Mystery of Tacit Knowledge and Release the Power of Innovation.* New York: Oxford University Press, 2000.

INDEX

complexity, 54–55; as double-edged sword, 1; emotions concerning, 1; envisioned, 116; having good ideas, 48–49; implementation dip, 49–51; innovation, 44–48; and leadership style, 39–40; managing, 42; and messiness, 41, 159; and moral purpose, 26; and organizational systems, 230–231; reculturing, 53–54; resistance, 52–53; top-down, 40; understanding, 4, 8, 39–76, 44–55; unfreezing, 39–40; views of, 43–44

Change leadership, components of, xv–xvi, 1–10

Chaos, xiv, 5, 59, 159; and complex systems, 55; moving toward the edge of, 160, 165

Charismatic leaders, 1–2; as strange attractors, 167, 174

Chesterton, G. K., xiv

Christmas tree schools, 44

Claxton, G., 186–188

Co-workers, treatment of, 78–79

Coaching leaders, 44; elements of, 51

Coercive leaders, 39–40, 58, 74; and emotional intelligence, 94; and implementation dips, 51; as listeners, 52

Cohen, D., 119

Coherence, 5, 9, 74, 159–184; assessment literacy, components of, 167–168; disturbance, creation of, 160–164; lateral accountability, 168, 174; living system, leading in, 160, 165; making, 166–169; and moral purpose, 22; as part of complexity, 6; persistent, 159–160; shared commitment, 169, 174; sorting, 169, 174

Collaborative cultures, 120–121; and knowledge sharing, 124–126

Collins, J., 80

Commitment, xiii; blind, 6; effective, outcome of, 7–8; external, 6–7; internal,

6–7, 199; of members, 6–7; shared, 169, 174

Communications trusts, 101–102, 103

Community, building a sense of, 225

Competence trust, 101, 103

Complexity, 166, 174, 202; success under conditions of, xiii–xiv

Complexity science, 54–55, 57; self-organizing, 166, 174; strange attractors, 166–167, 174

Complexity theory, core concepts of, 55

Components of change leadership, xv–xvi, 1–10; building relationships, 4; knowledge creation/organization, 4–5; making coherence, 5, 166–169; moral purpose, 4; understanding change, 4

Conflict, absence of, 97

Conger, J. A., 188, 201

Context setters, 162

Contractual trust, 101, 103

Courage, and culture of care, 122

Courage to Teach, The (Palmer), 25

Crisis, leadership in, 2–3

Culture, and moral purpose, 13

Culture of care, and knowledge, 122–132

Culture of change, developing new leaders for, 169

Culture of learning, 193

Culture of sharing, creating, 119–121

Customers, focusing on, 228–229; treatment of, 78–79

D

Daily learning, 169, 195–196

Darrah, C., 122

De Gues, A., 24

Deal, T., 26

Democratic leaders, 43; as listeners, 52

Dilemmas in leading change, 58

Dilke, Charles, 187

Dinkmeyer, D., 80

Havelock, R. G., 40

Heifetz, R., 2, 58, 98, 161, 200

Help access, and culture of care, 122

Hess, F. M., 161

Hesselbein, F., 221–222

High-trust cultures, 101

Homer-Dixon, T., 2, 201

How to Unlock the Mystery of Tacit Knowl-edge and Release the Power of Innova-tion (Von Krogh/Ichijo/Nonaka), 119

I

Ichijo, K., 119–120, 122, 124, 126, 127, 130, 197

Implementation dip, 49–51, 75–76

In Search of Excellence (Peters/Waterman), 58–59

Incoherence, attacking, 167

Individualized coaching, 192

Information, and people, 116

Innovation, 8, 161, 170; and change, 44–48

Instructional consulting services, 137–138, 141

Integrity, leading with, 11

Internal commitment, 6–7, 199

Intervisitation with peers, 133–136, 141, 192

Intracompany knowledge, harnessing, 129

J

Johnston, R., 221

Jones, G., 80

K

Keats, John, 187

King, B., 86

Knowledge: activation, 127; Assessment for Learning initiative, 138–139; creat-ing/sharing, 4–5, 9, 115–157, 169; and culture of care; dimensions of, 122–132; digestion of, 116; Early Years Literacy Project (EYLP), 140–141; ed-ucation examples, 133–142; enabling, 119; exchange, elements of, 126–130; explicit, 118; instructional consulting services, 137–138, 141; intervisitation and peer networks, 133–136, 141; in-tracompany; harnessing, 129; organi-zation, 4–5; as a social phenomenon, 115–122; tacit, 141; accessing, 118–119; turning information into, 5

Knowledge sharing, 169, 170; barriers to, 141; and collaborative culture, 124–126; conditions under which peo-ple share, 120; creating a culture of, 119–121; paradigm, 126

Knowledge society, use of term, 201

Kotter, J., 40, 119

Kouzes, J. M., 79–80

KPMG, 122

L

Lampel, J., 42

Larger community, making a contribu-tion to, 225–226

Lateral accountability, 168, 174

Leader to Leader series (Peter F. Drucker Foundation), 221–222

Leaders, *See also* Effective leaders; Leader-ship; Leadership styles; Leadership styles: character, 221–226; developing, 185–220; effective; and energy-enthu-siasm-hope constellation, 5–6; main mark of, 200; and moral purpose, 13–14; outcome of, 7–8; emotional in-telligence, 93–96; increasing the effec-tiveness of, 8; in knowledge-building organizations, 130; and moral pur-pose, 25; organizational values, 221–226; overly strong/directive, 200

Leading in a Culture of Change

MICHAEL FULLAN

$25.00 • Cloth • ISBN: 0-7879-5395-4

"*In* Leading in a Culture of Change, *Michael Fullan deftly combines his expertise in school reform with the latest insights in organizational change and leadership. The result is a compelling and insightful exposition on how leaders in any setting can bring about lasting, positive, systemic change in their organizations.*"

—John Alexander, president, Center for Creative Leadership

Business, nonprofit, and public sector leaders are facing new and daunting challenges—rapid-paced developments in technology, sudden shifts in the marketplace, and crisis and contention in the public arena. *Leading in a Culture of Change* offers new and seasoned leaders insights into the dynamics of change and presents a unique and imaginative approach for navigating the intricacies of the change process. Michael Fullan draws on the most current ideas and theories on the topic of effective leadership, incorporates case examples of large-scale transformation, and reveals a remarkable convergence of powerful themes or, as he calls them, the five core competencies.

By integrating these five core competencies—attending to a broader moral purpose, keeping on top of the change process, cultivating relationships, sharing knowledge, and setting a vision and context for creating coherence in organizations—leaders will be empowered to deal with complex change. They will be transformed into exceptional leaders who consistently mobilize their compatriots to do important and difficult work under conditions of constant change.

MICHAEL FULLAN (Toronto, Ontario) is Dean of the Ontario Institute for Studies in Education at the University of Toronto. He is recognized as an international authority on organizational change and is currently engaged in training, consulting, and evaluating organizational change projects around the world. He is the author of numerous books, including *Change Forces* and *The New Meaning of Educational Change.*